Riches to Rags

The Amazing and True Story of a Hungarian Mother's Escape to the West and Her Indomitable Courage

Susan Van Loon
Edited by Mike Yorkey

Copyright © 2012 by Susan Van Loon

Riches to Rags
The Amazing and True Story of a Hungarian Mother's
Escape to the West and Her Indomitable Courage
by Susan Van Loon

Printed in the United States of America

ISBN 9781624197864

All rights reserved solely by the author. The author guarantees all contents are original and do not infringe upon the legal rights of any other person or work. No part of this book may be reproduced in any form without the permission of the author. The views expressed in this book are not necessarily those of the publisher.

All *italics* regarding historical facts were taken from the Wikipedia, "History of Hungary"

Psychological disorders in *italics* taken from "Advances in Psychiatric Treatment" 2004, vol. 10

www.xulonpress.com

Table of Contents

Dedication

To my mother, Ann Szegedi, for her unconditional love and support. She is an inspiration to all mothers for her courage and strength in overcoming impossible hardships.

1

Unplanned Beginnings

*T*he year 1944 was not a good time to be living in Eastern Europe.

World War II was still raging, and in October of that year, Anikó and László Szegedi were forced to leave their apartment in Buda, Hungary, and flee the city. (Buda and Pest are separated by the Danube River, but the whole city is known as Budapest.)

They moved to Buda after their wedding on July 20, 1944, when László was a soldier in the Hungarian army in Pest. The newlyweds were only in their apartment for three short months before the warning sirens heralded the start of aerial bombardment. They hid in the basement of their apartment building, waiting for the terror to stop.

Terrible news was coming in from the Eastern cities. The Russians had moved into German-occupied Hungary and were headed toward Budapest, overtaking every city they crossed. They were barbarians with cruel hearts and absolutely no respect for human life. They were ravaging towns, smashing in doors of homes, and throwing families into the streets.

Young girls and women, pregnant or not, were brutally raped, and the fathers and husbands were often forced to watch. Sometimes they would all be killed after this atrocity.

In addition, the U.S. Army Air Force was carpet-bombing the country, and Budapest suffered the most blows. Anikó and László knew they had to flee out of the area. Little did they know that the siege of Budapest by the Russians, which started on November 3, 1944, would last until February 13, 1945, when the city fell.

During the siege, László was being deployed to a town near Balaton Lake, southwest of Budapest. As he was getting ready to leave, he told his wife, "Start packing, you're going with me! There is no way I'm leaving you alone, especially being three months pregnant."

"I can't really travel now," Anikó cried. "You know how sick I get every morning. But I know you are right, and I'm terrified at the idea of going through this by myself."

"Just get your things together. We'll manage somehow," replied László. "Hurry up! The Russians are quickly coming this way!"

They threw some clothes in a couple of suitcases, and off they went in a troop train with hundreds of other soldiers.

The town where the Hungarian soldiers were being deployed had to make room for all of them, so the soldiers randomly knocked at doors of peasant homes and ordered the owners to take in a couple of soldiers to live with them until further notice. Anikó and László stayed in one of these homes for many months. The conditions were not the best; they were cramped in a small home with the owners, but they made the best of the situation.

"Finally, I don't have morning sickness," exclaimed Anikó after staying two months in one particular home. "It has been so embarrassing, running to the outhouse four or five times a day!"

"You're getting quite a tummy on you. Is the baby kicking a lot?" László gently stroked her stomach.

"Oh, yes, he—or she—is quite active. I feel great, now that I'm past the halfway point."

When Anikó was eight-and-a-half months pregnant, László got orders to leave this small village and head to Austria because the Russians were closing in on them. Ironically, they left on April 4, 1945—the same day the "liberation" of Hungary from the Red Army took place. The fighting might have stopped, but Soviet forces sponsored the Communist government, so it was not true "liberation." Communism became the leading power and took over the country. Anikó and László did not find this out until several days later, however.

It hadn't been hard to pack—they just threw their clothes into two suitcases. As they walked outside, they were informed that they had been supplied with only one truck for fifty soldiers. The soldiers put all their belongings on the truck and started walking toward Austria, which was many kilometers from where they were, so they knew it would be several days of walking. The only two people in the truck were the driver and Anikó, who was getting close to delivering her baby.

The driver would constantly beg Anikó, "Please don't have this baby now. I know nothing about delivering babies."

"I still have a couple of weeks, so I think you're safe," she replied.

After walking for days, totally exhausted, the soldiers and the truck arrived in Graz, Austria, where they were stopped immediately by Austrian soldiers. They siphoned all the gasoline out of their truck since they needed to confiscate fuel for *their* tanks.

Anikó and László slept under their truck that first night for protection. Since it was the beginning of April, it was a very cold night, and they had to hold each other closely to keep warm. The next day László got an honorable discharge because of Anikó's condition, and all the other soldiers were relieved of their duties.

A farmer driving an old truck saw all the commotion from the soldiers dispersing in different directions. He noticed Anikó's protruding belly and approached them.

"Where are you headed? I can give you a ride if you're going toward Salzburg. I'm headed there anyway."

László was beyond thankful. "We would appreciate any help you can give us. We have no money, no food, and we are headed to Salzburg because we heard that a Hungarian refugee camp is there. We are hoping to get shelter for a while."

László and Anikó got into the truck reluctantly since it looked like it could fall apart at any moment.

"I'm so scared!" Anikó cried out to her husband. "What will happen to us? We have no money, and I'm so hungry. We haven't eaten in twenty-four hours!"

The truck driver had one hard-boiled egg, which he gave to László. László gave it to his wife, saying, "You eat this. This is all we have."

Anikó ate half the egg and insisted that László eat the other half. "You must eat something. Please eat the rest of the egg. You need your energy."

They had been on the road for three hours, and it was well past midnight.

Suddenly, they heard a huge bang, and the truck swerved out of control. They had lost a tire, and the truck slammed against some rocks, which stopped them from falling into a ditch.

"Help me!" Anikó cried out. "Something is happening to the baby!"

László saw the panic on Anikó's face and realized that she was probably going into labor. He gently helped her out of the truck, trying hard to remain calm. "Let's get out of here. We'll walk to that town down the road and try to get some help."

Anikó and László walked about a mile to the nearest town. Once in a while she had to stop because she was having labor pains that made her drop to her knees. As soon as the pain subsided, László helped her up and told her to hang on to him for support. She held up her belly, which was getting heavier by the minute. Seeing a tiny farmhouse getting closer and closer gave her the strength to go on.

They knocked at the door. A peasant woman opened it, looked at Anikó, and asked in German, "How far along are you?"

Anikó and László spoke German fluently. Anikó replied, "Almost nine months, and I believe I'm in labor. I'm having really bad pains."

"Don't worry, we have a midwife in town. I will go get her, but please allow your husband to come with me," pleaded the woman. "It is not safe for me to go alone. There are no lights in town because of the blackout."

Anikó lay on the cot in the kitchen, all alone in a strange house, in the middle of a war, in a strange country. She had to be in the dark so no attention would be drawn to the house, not knowing when help would arrive. The terror that filled her heart was almost more than she could bear. *What if László and the peasant woman do not return? They could get caught by the Russians and taken away.* Anikó just could not imagine giving birth to her baby without any help and no one to contact.

All she could do was pray, *Dear Lord, please help us and bring this little child into the world safely. Protect us through this uncertain time, and give us the strength we need now.*

After almost two hours, which felt like days, the woman of the house and László arrived with the midwife, who immediately went to work making Anikó more comfortable and advising her what to do when the time came. It was a long night, and as Anikó's pains got more intense, the more scared she became.

This was her first child, and there were no doctors around in case anything went wrong. Her desire to have a baby and to be a mother overcame all her fears and she knew she had to just bear the pain a little longer. László was pacing outside nervously since he could not endure staying in the house and would be of no use anyway.

After a long night, their little baby boy was born on April 9, 1945, as dawn welcomed another day. Miklós was a healthy little baby, and he immediately took to his mother's breast. Anikó, exhausted and still in shock over all they had endured, didn't know where they were.

"Please tell me the name of this town," she implored. "I would like to remember where my son was born."

"You are in St. Michael, and you and your family are safe," responded the peasant woman.

The next few days, Anikó had time to reflect on what had just happened. She gazed at her newborn son and wondered what the future held for him. She questioned if they could even survive this war.

This humble, impoverished entry into the world would hopefully not be symbolic of his life. As she held him close, feeding him, rocking him back and forth, she started thinking of her own childhood.

Things were so different then . . .

* * *

Anikó was one of five children born to a colonel in the Hungarian Army. She had three sisters and one brother. Her father, Zoltán Szilárd, was knighted and held high honors in the military. Two of her sisters were half-sisters from her father's first wife, Margit Sárkány.

Plaque honoring Zoltán Szilárd Knighting 1928
- Hungarian emblem upper right corner

Anikó's father, Colonel Zoltán Szilárd - 1928

Zoltán had fought bravely in World War I and was wounded five times. When he returned home and was reunited with Margit, he discovered that she had been unfaithful because she had contracted a sexually transmitted disease and passed it on to him. Unable to forgive her betrayal, Zoltán divorced her and married Anikó's mother, Erzsébet, some years later.

The Szilárds were a wealthy family and lived on a tree-shrouded ranch with horses, chickens, an orchard, and their own playground surrounded by beautiful flower gardens. Special quarters were next door for the help; they had nannies, housekeepers, and basically no worries in the world. Anikó learned to speak German from her German nanny, took piano lessons, loved to sing and dance, and had a wonderful free spirit about her.

Her father took a nap every afternoon, then left to spend hours at the Men's Club, smoking cigars and playing cards with the other members. Her mother stayed at home and raised the five children. Several times a week, Erzsébet would play bridge with her friends.

One of Anikó's sisters, Éva, was an extremely outgoing and bubbly person who loved life. When she was seventeen, she was learning how to dive at the public pool. Although she was an excellent swimmer, she just couldn't bring herself to dive headfirst into the water. A good-looking man in his early thirties was sitting at the side of the pool. Éva, who was quite flirtatious, swam up to him and asked,

"Sir, would you teach me how to dive? I just can't seem to get it."

"Of course, young lady, *this* is the way you dive!" László Varsányi responded. Within moments, he performed the most beautiful swan dive Èva had ever seen.

Èva, being sassy and young, teased him. "*This* is the way you dive, young man. Watch this!"

She tried her best to perform a swan dive, but she did a great belly flop instead. He started laughing at her clumsiness, and as she came out of the water, she laughed along with him, not embarrassed in the least. She sat next to him and learned that he had a serious nature. He was a captain in the Hungarian army and was very disciplined in everything he did. They talked for hours, told stories about themselves, and agreed to meet again the next day.

This chance meeting grew into a passionate romance, and they dated for several months after which they were married. Èva and her husband were extremely happy, but they only had a short time together. She conceived immediately after the wedding, and although her husband was a captain in the army, he had to go back to his post. He returned a year later to see his child for the first time, stayed long enough to impregnate Èva again, and then he went back to fighting in Russia. He was discharged in 1944 and was returning home when the troop train was bombed, killing him. He died before he could see his second child.

Anikó's grandfather on her dad's side was an evangelical pastor in the town of Domony, Hungary.

Her dad's sister was married to a Lutheran pastor in the town of Domony as well.

When Anikó was thirteen years old, her parents sent her to live with Uncle George and his wife for three months during the summer, a time she spent preparing for confirmation in the Lutheran church. She studied the Bible extensively and became a strong Christian. Before confirmation, the children stood in front of hundreds of people in church and had to answer several questions from the Bible. The preparation gave Anikó a solid foundation in the Christian faith that sustained her for the rest of her life.

She was raised in a strict home. Her father, a colonel, made sure they had good manners, knew how to behave in public, and knew the etiquette for every social situation.

When Anikó was about eight, she was taking a bath when her father came into the bathroom and reprimanded her. "Don't you hear what they are playing on the radio?" Colonel Szilárd demanded. "They are playing the Hungarian national anthem! You get up and stand at attention when you hear any country's anthem played, especially yours! Do you understand?"

Anikó jumped up and stood naked in the bathtub while the anthem played on the radio.

Anikó and her siblings had to do everything according to the rules, and as long as they obeyed, they had no problems. Living on a beautiful ranch with a fruit orchard, she recalled how much fun she and her siblings had climbing the cherry and apple trees and eating the fresh fruit. They loved to play in the large sandbox, and since there were five of them, there was always someone to play with.

After she finished middle school, Anikó's parents sent her to a teacher's college for two years, where she also took piano lessons. She lived in a dorm with other girls and had the time of her life. Her brother, Zoltán, Jr., was sent to a military school at the age of ten to make a man out of him, and since his father was a military man, they wanted to steer Zoli in that direction. But as he grew older, he had no interest in the military. Instead, he loved swimming and started training daily.

Colonel Zoltán Szilárd and son, Zoli at ten
at his military Academy

After Anikó turned sixteen, she went to dances several times a year, chaperoned by her father, of course. The dances were held in large ballrooms where the girls always wore long formal gowns, and the boys wore pressed suits. After a couple of these dances, Anikó met several friends she loved to dance with. At one of the dances, her father, who was seated up in the balcony, counted fifteen young men who asked Anikó to dance during one song.

He told her, "You're getting more and more popular at these dances. Seems like most of the boys want to dance with you!"

"I love to dance, Father! Thank you for bringing me here tonight. This is so much fun!" She gave him a big hug and kiss. "I can hardly wait for the next one."

As far as having any interest in cooking or anything to do with household chores, Anikó had none. She didn't have to prepare any meals because, after all, they had cooks to do that. She had no intention of ever walking into the kitchen to learn how to cook.

Anikó at 19, graduation picture

Her sister, Ėva, on the other hand, was always hanging around the kitchen and wanting to know how everything was prepared. At age eighteen, Anikó had no idea how to even boil water and didn't realize how useful a talent for cooking would become later in life for her and her family.

* * *

Meanwhile, her future husband László was fortunate to have come from a wealthy family as well. His grandfather was the editor and owner of a newspaper in Debrecen. His father was the CEO of the engineering company, also in Debrecen. He designed the streetcar system for the whole city, for which he received great recognition and compensation.

László had one brother and two sisters who all went to the finest schools in the country. He loved poetry and writing, quite opposite of his father, who was an engineer. László took after his grandfather when he became a journalist.

The head of a major newspaper in Budapest, Vitéz Kolozsvári Borcsa Mihály, promised László a great future in the newspaper business. He promised to make László a newspaper editor in Berlin after the war was over, which gave him hope for the future.

László, who lived in Budapest at the time, wrote a play that was presented in Debrecen, and Anikó had a dancing part in it. Anikó was only seventeen, and László was twenty-three years old. Right after the play, they had a celebration dance for all the participants.

László walked up to Anikó and asked, "May I dance with you?"

Anikó was a very beautiful young lady with big blue eyes, curly blonde hair, and an attractive slim figure. She was quite honored to get a chance to dance with the writer of the play, so she replied, "Of course, I would love to dance with you."

As they danced, all he could talk about was poetry and writing, which bored her to tears. She walked up to some of her other dancing partners and begged them, "Please fill my dance card so I don't have to dance with that writer!"

László was not giving up, however. He was persistent in wanting to know her, so he succeeded in dancing with her three more times. On each occasion, he tried to charm her with his poetic magic.

They did not see each other for six months until one day when László was in Debrecen, he saw her at the country club pool, and walked up to her.

"Do you remember me? We danced last year after the play," he said.

She vaguely remembered him, and since they had already met once, she thought it would be all right to speak to him. They saw each other every single day for one week, but this time around, they fell madly in love. He returned to Budapest, and they corresponded by mail, daily for a year, except for a few occasional visits he could make to Debrecen.

After a year and a half, he asked Anikó to marry him, and of course she said yes, anticipating a beautiful life ahead of them. They were married at St.

Anne's Catholic Church in Debrecen on July 20, 1944. She was a beautiful bride with a white satin dress that was embroidered with lace and pearls and had a long train that flowed after her as she walked.

As for László, he was a handsome groom, tall and slender with jet-black hair. They arrived at the church in a horse and buggy, decorated with beautiful flowers. There were about twenty guests, including family members, several journalists, and the head of a newspaper in Budapest.

Anikó and László's wedding, July 20th, 1944

Anikó in her wedding gown entering St. Anne's Church

Anikó's sister, Èva, attended but was somber and dressed in black. She was twenty years old with two children, mourning the death of her husband and recalling her own wedding just a few years before. Now she was a widow and had to depend on her parents to help with raising her children.

Even though Anikó's mother had never talked to her about the birds and the bees, she had a good idea what would happen on the wedding night, but she had no inkling that she would have to have sex on a regular basis the rest of her life. She did not have any experience with the opposite sex and was a virgin, so this was all new to her.

The subject of sex was not brought up in the 1930s and 1940s in upper middle-class families. This was something you learned on your own as well as to be submissive to your husband's needs. Their honeymoon was in a town in southeast Hungary, which is now Transylvania. László shocked her on the first day of their honeymoon as he turned out to be quite the lover. Now that Anikó had discovered what sex was all about, she looked forward to the next time, which wasn't too far away with her new husband.

Anikó and László had an apartment waiting for them in Buda since László worked close by in Pest. They had their place beautifully furnished. Anikó had a grand piano that her parents had given her because she loved to play whenever she had the chance. For a few months, they had a wonderful romantic relationship, except for the occasional interruption of the sirens warning of another bombing attack. When they heard the sirens, they had to rush down to the basement from the third floor, using the stairs since they could not use the elevator in case their building got hit.

After missing her first menstrual cycle and feeling extremely nauseous in the mornings, Anikó knew she had conceived on their wedding night.

"What? You're pregnant?" László could not believe his ears when Anikó told him of her condition. "That is wonderful. I'm so happy!"

Anikó was thrilled as well to have a baby. "I love you so much, and now we will have our baby to show our love for each other," she said. She jumped into his arms, and they hugged and kissed for a long time. The young couple did not even consider their situation, being in the middle of a war. They were both ecstatic with the news.

For the next three months, she would vomit several times a day. At night, they would run to the bomb shelter, and when they came back from below, she would vomit again from the stress.

* * *

Anikó snapped out of her daydreaming, and then the reality of their situation hit hard. In the midst of all these difficult circumstances, she actually felt blessed that God had led them to this little farmhouse. If they had not had a blowout, they would have been stuck in the middle of nowhere when the baby was born.

As she recalled the events of how they were led to the farmhouse, she compared their situation to that of Mary and Joseph, who ended up in a manger because there was no room at the inn.

They stayed with the peasant woman for a couple of weeks. She insisted on taking care of them until Anikó could regain her strength. László went every day to the Hungarian army headquarters so they would have some food to live on since the peasant woman had no means to feed them *and* herself.

They decided to take the train to Salzburg, so they left St. Michael and headed to a Hungarian camp, where the Austrians had facilities for them. Anikó's only priority at this point was to take care of her newborn son under any circumstances.

* * *

February, March, and April 1945 were full of many world events. The Soviets launched a massive assault against German-occupied Hungary towards the end of October 1944, which lasted until the fall of Budapest in February 1945. Also in February, the Soviets invaded Silesia and Pomerania, while Western Allied forces entered Western Germany close to the Rhine River. In March, the Western Allies crossed the Rhine north and south of the Ruhr, encircling a large number of German troops, while the Soviets advanced to Vienna and captured it in April. In early April, the Western Allies finally pushed forward in Italy and swept across Western Germany, while Soviet forces stormed Berlin in late April. The two forces linked up on the Elbe River on April 25. On April 30, 1945, the Reichstag was captured, signaling the military defeat of the Third Reich.

Several changes in leadership occurred during this period. On April 12, U.S. President Franklin Delano Roosevelt died and was succeeded by Harry Truman. Benito Mussolini was killed by Italian partisans on April 28. Two days later, Hitler committed suicide and was succeeded by Grand Admiral Karl Dönitz. German forces surrendered in Italy on April 29 and in Western Europe on May 7. On the Eastern Front, Germany surrendered to the Soviets on May 8, 1945.

World War II altered the political alignment and social structure of the world. The Soviet Union and the United States emerged as rival superpowers, setting the stage for the Cold War.

* * *

Anikó and László bravely faced their situation, but they were both frightened by what the future might bring for them. When they arrived at the Hungarian camp, they were given cots to sleep on and food to eat.

After the second month in the refugee camp, Anikó asked László, "How much longer do we have to stay here? I have no idea what has happened to our family back home!"

"You know, we could just stay out here in Austria and not go back to Hungary," László told his wife. "After all this blows over, we could go to America and start a new life."

Anikó considered the possibility for a while and then answered, "It is very tempting, I'm sure we would be better off, but what about all our family back home? We don't even know if anyone is alive! We have a tiny baby, and I'm scared to start such a journey with Miklós so small. If we didn't have him, I would seriously consider it."

The next day, they were put on a train with other Hungarian refugees to be sent back to Budapest since the Austrians could not take care of thousands of refugees any longer. The Austrians had problems of their own.

Anikó and László got on the train with their little son and headed toward Budapest, not knowing what they would find, or what lay ahead for them. The dirty conditions on the train made Anikó even more protective of her baby, and she tried to shield him from any harm. This train was normally used to carry animals and cargo, so it wasn't the most sterile environment.

She gathered the water from the steam coming out of the engine to bathe her son and washed his diapers in the same water. The smell of the coal coming from the locomotive permeated the air, prompting Anikó to think of how damaging this could be to her tiny baby. The train ride took four long days, and it stopped frequently for hours at a time.

There was an old Hungarian wives' tale that if you ate caraway soup, it would build more milk in your body for breastfeeding. Every chance she had, she cooked caraway soup outside the coach when they stopped at a train station. She wanted to have enough food for Miklós. Most of the women cooked while the train stopped, the men made a fire next to the train, and then they would put together a make-shift tripod. The women hung their pots—which they always carried with them—over the fire, and cooked with whatever ingredients they had.

Before they arrived in Budapest, the Hungarian conductor stopped the train and informed them, "The Russians are waiting for you in Budapest, and they are planning to arrest all of you for fleeing the country illegally!"

Everyone got off the train and scattered in different directions, including László and Anikó with their infant son.

The train arrived empty at the Budapest train station.

2

Destruction and Devastation

*A*s Anikó and László worked their way back to their apartment on foot, on streetcars, and any way they could, they witnessed much destruction along the way. Budapest was in shambles.

Buildings had been bombed, houses burned and destroyed, and people were running back and forth in a panic, not knowing what to do next. The entire city suffered complete chaos from destruction of the worst kind.

As they approached their apartment building, László yelled out, "Look at our place. It's been hit!"

Anikó almost collapsed at the sight of their home having been destroyed, but there was a glimmer of hope. "Look up there! Our apartment is still halfway intact. Let's get some workers to check if there is anything we can salvage."

László thought that was a great idea, so they approached several men working on the street and asked if they could help them recover anything left in their apartment.

The men agreed to help out and climbed up a broken-down stairway to assess the damage. When they came back down, they informed László about their findings.

"Sir, there is still some furniture and kitchenware intact, but the labor to salvage your belongings will cost you something. What can you pay us?"

"We have no money."

"Then we'll need the grand piano in payment."

Anikó gasped. "I love my piano, but if we have to give it away, then so be it."

László felt sorry for his wife since he knew how much Anikó loved to play the piano. They realized that they could keep only their most important and useful belongings.

The worker added, "There's a candy dish that fell off the coffee table, but it looks like it has minimal damage."

The candy dish Anikó and László received
as a wedding present from head of the newspaper

Anikó remembered the expensive porcelain candy dish they had received as a wedding gift from the head of the newspaper. She asked if they could please get that back, as well as any other undamaged items.

Anikó also had two complete boxes of Herendi china in her dowry, never opened, but those heirlooms had been blown to bits. Herendi, a famous and valuable china, was created by the Hungarians and had been produced for centuries.

The landlord of their apartment building told László that he had to be careful. "You're on the 'wanted list' for writing against Communism. They've been looking for you," he said. He informed them that the head of the newspaper, Vitéz Kolozsvári Borcsa Mihály (who was the best man at their wedding), had been hanged for writing against Communism and the advance of the Red Army.

The news devastated László, and he realized that his future in the newspaper business was over since he would never join the Communist regime. László would rather see his family starve than betray what he believed in.

Anikó's hopes of a great future had been wiped away. She had been dreaming of being the wife of a newspaper editor in Berlin and raising children in freedom, but now that was all shattered. As the reality of their situation hit home, Anikó questioned the whereabouts of their loved ones.

"Where are my sisters and brother? Where are my parents?" she asked László. He had no answer for her. He was also wondering the same thing about his family.

The whole country was in an upheaval. The trains were arriving in Budapest from the East, where people's homes and towns had been either destroyed or captured by the Soviets. Anikó later learned that her parents had been forced out of their beautiful home and were on one of these trains fleeing for their lives in April 1945.

Anikó's father, being a colonel in the Hungarian Army, had become an enemy of the government. He and his family set off for Austria, where they were informed in Passau that the war was over and they needed to get off the train. They were escorted to a Hungarian camp where they stayed until they were shipped back to their country.

Anikó's brother, Zoli, was fifteen years old when he and his buddies from the military school decided that they would go to Austria to find his parents. They walked to Austria and wandered around for several weeks before they found Zoli's parents. The boys were hungry, filthy, and extremely tired.

Anikó's mother, Erzsébet, started reading tarot cards and foretelling the future because she had heard there was a lot of interest among the people. Erzsébet had tried fortune-telling for the fun of it before, but she never thought in her wildest dreams that people would give her money or barter items to have their tarot cards read. She was soon bartering for food — eggs, fruit, bread, or anything else they could get through her tarot cards. Erzsébet's actions saved her family from starvation.

Zoli would tell his mother, "Hurry and start reading the cards. I'm hungry."

Their lifestyle had changed after the Russians had confiscated their beautiful sixty-acre ranch out in the country, where they had horses, dogs, and nannies. Now they experienced poverty at its worst, as did many Hungarian families with property. The Red Army swept through the country, overtaking territories, forcing people out of their homes, and killing them if they showed any resistance.

Anikó's mother and father returned to Hungary with Zoli after a few weeks, and since they had no home, they found refuge at the home of Anikó's uncle, who lived near Budapest. He was a schoolteacher, so the Soviets did not take his house from him. To survive, Anikó's mother had to get a job carrying heavy mortar for a cement company. This was not easy for a woman who had been pampered all her life and never did any physical labor. Anikó's father was eighteen years older than her mother, so there was nothing he could do to help.

Meanwhile, Anikó and László really didn't know where they could go at this point. Then Anikó found out that the Russians had taken her parents' house along with sixty acres of land. She still had no idea what had happened to them, but she knew they could not go back to her parents' house. Her father's first wife lived in Budapest, and she offered to store all their leftover belongings from their apartment until they could find a place to live.

Severe Inflation

The Hungarian forint was losing its value daily because of serious inflation in the country. Even doctors had to barter for food or whatever they could get.

László's parents were forced to move from their home as well, but they were fortunate enough to move in with their daughter, Kató, and her husband, Karcsi. They lived in a small town called Mórágy, and as soon as László found out his parents were living with his sister, he decided to look them up, hoping for refuge.

László's brother-in-law, Karcsi, was a family doctor, so they were still relatively well off since he was the only doctor around for several towns in the near vicinity. The town of Mórágy was fully populated when they arrived and consisted of mainly German-speaking Hungarians called Swabians. What a relief it was when László and Anikó knocked at their door, and Kató and Karcsi welcomed them with open arms!

Kató cried out, "Oh, my God, it is so good to see you! We had no idea what had happened, especially with Anikó expecting. Please come in and let us look at this beautiful baby boy."

László was grateful to be reunited with his parents, sister, and brother-in-law. They all lived together for several months and shared their adventures about how they all had escaped harm from the Russians and the bombings.

"We may have to stay in this town for a few years," László explained. "The Communists are looking for me because of my writings." He also told his wife, "I have to change my name, too. Otherwise, they will find me for sure. From now on, I will go by the name of Miklós since there is no record of him in Hungary."

"How are we going to live if you can't work?" Anikó asked.

The whole family had a meeting that night. The town pastor was there as well, and he told them there was no one to teach the school of fifty children. Since Anikó had a degree in teaching, everyone in the family decided that the best thing for her to do would be to start teaching. She had no choice in the matter. Miklós was just a little baby and she needed to care for him, but she realized that this would be the best solution under the circumstances.

They moved into a small, abandoned farmhouse with dirt floors and no plumbing or electricity, just lanterns.

"This is quite different from our beautiful apartment in Budapest," observed Anikó. "But at least it's a roof over our heads."

Since there were no jobs for him to do, László decided to write and direct a play in the town. Obviously, he wasn't paid for his time. He enjoyed writing, so he spent his days writing and directing the play, not really worrying about how his family was going to survive. In his spare time, he would write articles, mainly against Communism, but they ended up in a drawer. He had to get his anger and frustration out, and the only way he was able to achieve that was with a pen and paper.

László was suffering from a form of depression, and the only thing that relaxed him was his writing. It hurt him terribly that he could not be a journalist, which he felt was his calling.

Anikó started teaching fifty children, all in one classroom. Within a few months, however, the number of students had dropped to twenty since most of the German townspeople had been forced by the German authorities to flee to Austria. The Communist government then decided to "help" the homeless people from the surrounding towns. They brought them to Mórágy and told them they could move into the nice homes that had been abandoned. The Communist officials also told them to remember how good the government was to them for taking from the rich and giving all this property to the poor.

One problem the government didn't consider was the reason why these people were poor in the first place. Many were homeless because they were lazy. After moving in, they could have worked the land, taken care of the vineyards and had nice wineries, but they didn't. They could have taken care of the animals, but they didn't, so all the animals died off. Within a couple of years they all moved out and preferred to be homeless again so they wouldn't have to do any work on the farms. The town became a ghost town, and all the farmland was abandoned.

László could have worked in a vineyard too since there was one next door, but the thought never occurred to him since physical labor was beneath him. He could have easily turned the vineyard into a moneymaking venture. Instead, he stayed with

Miklós until Anikó came home, and he would cook dinner once in a while.

Another One on the Way

Within a few months after Anikó started teaching, she started feeling nauseous in the mornings. She had a strange feeling about what could be causing it.

Good Lord, could I be pregnant again? This is not what we need now! I have to keep working. What am I to do?

She and László discussed their situation that night, and they agreed that she would continue to work until the school year was over and then prepare for the baby to be born.

Anikó's parents and Zoli came and stayed with them for a few months since they had no home to go to. Anikó now had some help with the chores and cooking.

On the morning of August 10, 1946, Anikó was doing laundry and hanging clothes on the clothesline when she started having labor pains. She knew it was her time.

She yelled for her brother, Zoli. "Hurry and get Karcsi and ask him to come over! I need help with the delivery of this baby!"

Karcsi wasn't an obstetrician, but he would have to do. The labor pains did not last long, and by noon she had given birth to a healthy baby girl who they named Zsuzsi. Sixteen-year-old Zoli, who was not allowed to stay in the house to watch, went outside and climbed a tree so he would have a good view of the room where Anikó was delivering. He got a first-hand lesson regarding childbirth, which disgusted him.

Soon after Zsuzsi was born, Anikó's parents and Zoli moved close to Budapest to a relative's house due to the tight living quarters.

All the years while Anikó and László were struggling to survive, Zoli was training to swim in the Olympics. His only passion was for this sport. He spent many hours a day perfecting his strokes, not realizing what was going on around him or that his sister's family was near starvation. His drive to become a great swimmer blinded him because he was determined to be in the Olympics and swim for Hungary at all costs.

Anikó and László were thrilled with their new baby girl, but they also realized that they couldn't go on having babies under such tenuous circumstances.

School began in September, and Anikó had to go back to work. She took Zsuzsi in a baby buggy every day to the school a few blocks away, while Miklós stayed at home with László. She put Zsuzsi in the principal's office while she was teaching, and the principal's wife took care of her. At recess, Anikó breastfed her little baby and could hardly wait for the school day to be over so she could spend some time with her children.

Life was not easy, and this is not what she had in mind when she married László. What a twist of fate! Now she was the breadwinner of the family, and her husband was at home, not working at all. Sure, he helped with dinner from time to time, but most of the responsibilities of cleaning, cooking, and washing clothes still fell on Anikó's shoulders. She never wanted to teach either because this was not something she enjoyed. She wanted to stay home with her two children.

Miklós was a little jealous of his baby sister, who got to go with Mommy to school and received more attention. Since they had no electricity, they cooked with a wood-burning stove. As the fire burned out, only warm ashes were left.

One day, when Miklós was only eighteen months old, he decided to "bury" his baby sister, so he started piling ashes on Zsuzsi's face. He thought it was cute the way she sputtered and coughed until László came in the room and caught him. Miklós didn't think it was so cute after his dad disciplined him.

Zsuzsi and Miklós, ages 1 and 2

Two years passed, and nothing really changed. Miklós was over three years old, and Zsuzsi had turned two. Miklós would often go next door to play with the neighbor boy, whose father was a carpenter. Miklós was learning all kinds of new dirty words from his playmate—words that he didn't know the meaning of. He came up with some words that even Anikó had never heard of, so she had to ask László what they meant.

One day, Miklós walked up to his little sister and said, "You stinking little whore." Anikó sure knew the meaning of that sentence, and she and László had to sit down with Miklós and tell him that those were bad words and not to use them again. Another day, Miklós had just come back from playing next door, and as he was circling the kitchen table, he mumbled something. All Anikó could see was his curly blond hair above the edge of the table as he was bouncing up and down. She got a little closer to listen to what he was saying.

"Pussy, pussy, pussy," he said. Once again, he had picked up bad language from next door.

Both of Miklós' grandfathers were from upper-class families, and cussing was not tolerated. The next time the grandfathers came to visit, Anikó mentioned that Miklós had been picking up some very bad language next door. Her father asked, "Can we just sit here and listen to what he has to say?"

Soon enough, Miklós started reciting some of his new vocabulary, and both grandfathers laughed so hard they had tears in their eyes. His grandfather would tell Miklós, "Come on, say that again. What was that?"

Anikó stepped in. "What are you trying to do, teach him to say bad words? Stop it!"

"But he is so cute when he says them," her father said. "Let us have a little fun. He will outgrow it soon."

Anikó really loved her two children, and it just broke her heart that she could not stay home and spend quality time with them. Besides having a full-time job teaching, she had to do all the cooking and cleaning since László was doing less and less. To cook, she had to build a fire in the stove, then go outside and draw the water from the well, sometimes in the dead of winter. Every meal was made from scratch. Clothes had to be hand washed in tubs, and dirty diapers had to be boiled since there was no washing machine.

One day, tired and depressed, Anikó approached László and told him, "I cannot stand this pace anymore. I'm exhausted, and all the responsibility is on my head. This is not fair. I cannot work under these conditions, and my children need their mother!"

His immediate reply was, "If you don't work, then we don't eat!" This left such a permanent wound in her heart that she could never feel the same way about him as she did before.

* * *

On February 1, 1946, Hungary was declared a republic, and the leader of the Smallholders, Zoltán

Tildy, became President, handing over the office of Prime Minister to Ferenc Nagy.

Mátyás Rákosi, leader of the Communist Party, became deputy Prime Minister. The Communists exercised constant pressure on the Smallholders, both inside and outside the government, nationalizing industrial companies, banning religious civil organizations, and occupying key positions in local public administration. Socialism was declared the main goal of the nation. A new coat-of-arms was adopted with Communist symbols: the red star, the hammer, and the sickle.

Mátyás Rákosi now attempted to impose totalitarian rule on Hungary. The centrally orchestrated personality cult focused on him and Stalin soon reached unprecedented proportions. Rákosi's images and busts were everywhere. All public speakers were required to glorify his wisdom and leadership. By 1950, the state controlled most of the economy, such as all large and mid-sized industrial companies, plants, mines, banks of all kinds, and all companies of retail and foreign trade. All were nationalized without any compensation.

The government ordered ever-higher requirements of compulsory food quotas on peasants' produce. Rich peasants, called "kulaks," were declared "class enemies" and suffered all sorts of discrimination, including imprisonment and loss of property. With them, some of the most able farmers were removed from production. The declining agricultural output led to a constant scarcity of food, especially meat.

Rákosi rapidly expanded the education system in Hungary. This was in attempt to replace the educated class of the past with what Rákosi called a "new working intelligentsia." In addition to efforts such as better education for the poor, there were more opportunities for the working class. While this increased literacy in general, the measure also disseminated Communist ideology in schools and universities. Also, as part of an effort to separate the church from the state, nearly all religious schools were taken into state ownership. Religious instruction was denounced as retrograde propaganda and was gradually eliminated from schools.

It didn't take too long for the Hungarian people to realize that socialism did not work! It killed the human spirit and took away all their incentives for free enterprise.

Life Goes On

For three years, László did not earn any money, and Anikó was tired of the whole mess. She asked for a transfer close to Budapest, which she received. It was a new job teaching in Gödöllõ, a town just a few kilometers from Budapest.

She told László, "It might be easier for you to get some work since this will be closer to Budapest. There must be someplace you can work." Also, her parents were not too far away from Gödöllõ, so they could help with the children when necessary.

They moved to a small house that was part of the elementary school, which made everything convenient for her and the kids. Finally, they could get their salvaged furniture back from Pest, where it had been stored for the last three years. As they arranged the furniture and opened each box, they were thrilled with each familiar piece as they placed them around their tiny house.

László finally found a job with a printing company, but as soon as the company found out who he was, he was fired immediately. He was told that he should be happy that he was only being fired because his whereabouts could be reported to the Communists and he would be thrown in jail. László took the streetcar to Budapest every day to look for a job, but nothing was forthcoming. He had to be careful every time he stepped out in public.

Again, all the responsibility of the family was on Anikó's shoulders, and now she was alone with her kids most of the time. László always had reasons why he had to stay in the city, and quite frankly, Anikó was getting tired of his excuses. Sometimes she questioned his whereabouts. She knew if she didn't work, they would probably starve. Carrying that burden wore on her.

She tended a small vegetable garden, which helped feed her children. She also taught piano lessons in the late afternoons. She had seven students, and instead of being paid money, she bartered for fruit. In the summer, her children were fed fresh fruits and vegetables, but not too much meat since that was scarce. They were lucky if they had meat a couple of times a month.

In the winter, the parents of her students gave her sausage and pork cuts because that's when they would slaughter the pigs. It was wonderful to have more meat in the wintertime. At the end of the summer, Anikó had so many plums from bartering that she canned them. She would stay awake all night making jam and putting the fruit preserves in jars. After a few hours of sleep, she went off to school to teach. It was nice to know that when winter came, her family would have fruit.

There were a few incidences that really jarred Anikó and László's hearts. Miklós was about five when he came home from kindergarten and told them, "The great Russian leader, Lenin, is my father!"

This is what he was taught in school, and hearing this devastated Anikó. She took Miklós by the hand, walked him over to László, pointed at him, and said, "This is your father, not Lenin. You have to love your daddy, not that other man!"

Another incident that happened in school actually amused her. One day, as Anikó was talking to one of the ten-year-old students, he started sharing with her about his conversation with his dad the night before.

"My daddy told me that Stalin croaked, so they cut him open and stuffed his guts with dirty rags!"

Anikó could hardly hold back the laughter. Trying to compose herself, she realized that if she had turned the father in to the authorities, he could have been jailed for a minimum of six months for saying what he did. So Anikó told the little boy, "I'm so glad you told me about this, but this has to be our secret. Do not tell anyone else about this, okay?"

Sunday mornings, Anikó was required to take the students to "free movies," which were propaganda films about what a great socialist country Hungary was. According to the government the children needed to appreciate what their country was giving them.

One of the titles was, *You Have to be a Good Party Member*. Every movie had some sort of Communistic propaganda that was seeking to brainwash the little children. At the time she took the students to the movies, the local church bells rang out. Hearing those bells broke Anikó's heart since it was not advisable to go to church if she wanted to keep her job.

When Miklós and Zsuzsi were about five and six, Anikó and László decided to go to church on Easter Sunday anyway. They figured going once a year wouldn't cause too much harm, and they wanted their children to experience what church was all about. Monday morning, as soon as Anikó walked into school, she was asked to go to the principal's office.

"Yesterday, at the Communist Party meeting, it was discussed that you and your family went to church yesterday," the principal said. "I've been ordered to fire you first thing today, but I refused. You have no idea how I had to fight to save your job! Please do me a favor. If you decide to go to church again, go to another town where they don't know you."

Living as Paupers

Anikó and László were so poor while they lived in Gödöllő that there were days when Anikó had to get creative about what to make for dinner. She was making 540 forints a month, a small amount to support four people, and László was not bringing too much money home. László's parents had moved back to Debrecen, and they were starting to do very well again, but they never offered to help their son who was in dire need.

One day, when László's parents came to visit, László's mother pulled out a sweater she had just bought and showed it to Anikó. "Look what a wonderful deal I got on this sweater," she exclaimed. "It only cost me 700 forints."

Anikó's heart sank. She thought to herself, *You bitch. I make less than that in one month, and I support your son and two grandchildren with that money.*

She thought about the two dresses she owned and the one pair of shoes her daughter owned. When Zsuzsi's feet grew, Anikó had to cut out the toes of the shoes so that they would last longer since the family could not afford another pair of shoes.

Besides having a brother-in-law who was a doctor, László had another brother-in-law who was a veterinarian. He boasted to Anikó that he made 16,000 forints per month. Anikó was put in her place and realized that they were the paupers of the family. He told her, "I'd offer to help you, but I know László would never try to get a job." There was a bit of truth in what he said.

For lunch, Miklós and Zsuzsi would eat bread with lard on it and were thankful when they would have a piece of bell pepper to flavor it. Zsuzsi would sit at lunchtime and smell the aroma of the salami that her classmates had on their sandwiches.

One day, a little girl offered Zsuzsi a piece of her salami. Zsuzsi took it, broke it up into small pieces, and spread it out on her lard sandwich so she could savor the taste in every bite.

Zsuzsi and Miklós at 6 and 7

Anikó always made sure that her children were given nutritious meals, as best as she could provide. She was so concerned about her family that she forgot to take care of herself. She hadn't eaten a healthy diet when she was pregnant, and since she wasn't able to take care of herself like she should have, her body was showing signs of malnutrition.

She started getting boils all over her body and could not understand why.

Anikó had scurvy, a disease caused by vitamin C deficiency due to the lack of fruits and vegetables in her diet. Red blisters on the body, bleeding of the gums, loose teeth, joint pain, and muscle aches are symptoms of scurvy, and Anikó had them all. She realized that if she didn't take better care of herself, her children would not be cared for.

Anikó always put her family first. She had wanted to make sure everyone else had enough nourishment, but now her body was deteriorating due to her sacrifices. She had to do something about it, and that's when Anikó decided to take better care of herself for her children's sake. She also decided that she would sit and rest every day for a while to regain her strength. Plus, this way she could watch her children play.

One autumn day, when Zsuzsi and Miklós were about six and seven, a neighbor girl was given a pretty new doll for her birthday. She came over to show the doll to Zsuzsi, like most school girls would.

"Look at my pretty doll," her friend said. "You don't have one like it, na-na na-na na-na."

Her friend was right. Zsuzsi didn't have *any* dolls because her parents could not afford even one.

Miklós and Zsuzsi had been catching flies and killing them, so Zsuzsi's only comeback was, "We have dead flies, and you don't. Na-na na-na na-na."

When Anikó saw this happening, it broke her heart. She promised herself that someday her children would have a good life and get beautiful presents, no matter what she had to do to achieve it!

Miklós and Zsuzsi, at 8 and 9

Miklós and Zsuzsi were very close, and Miklós was protective of his little sister. They walked to school together, and Miklós stood up to any bullies who tried to torment his sister. They were about nine and seven when one day after school, three tough boys grabbed Miklós and pinned him against a pole. Some of the boys were jealous of Miklós and Zsuzsi because their mother was the schoolteacher, and Miklós earned better grades than them since he studied hard and even spent recesses with a friend doing schoolwork.

Two of the boys held his hands behind the pole while the third one picked up a shovel and raised it over his head. The implement came down with a swift blow against Miklós, but the shovel struck him in the chin. If the shovel had hit him in the neck, he would have been killed instantly.

Zsuzsi was looking for her brother so they could walk home together when she saw what happened. "Please don't hurt him! Somebody help!"

Two of the boys then held her down, and made her watch as the other bully struck her brother again. She was helpless. She tried fighting the boys, but they started hitting her. There was nothing she could do, but scream.

When the boys saw the blood gushing out of Miklós' chin, they realized how badly they had hurt him and ran away. Zsuzsi helped her brother get back home. Anikó was shocked at what happened, but she could not do anything about the situation because she could lose her job. Some of the boys had parents who were important party members, so there was nothing she could do but suffer in silence.

Anikó was despondent about her situation, especially the fact she had to teach within the Communist regime rules. She was not allowed to speak about God at school, or anything against the socialist rulers. Each day when class began, she had to lead the class in a chant dictated by the authorities of the Communist Party.

"Elõre!" they would say in unison. *Forward!*

Anikó had to be two-faced in what she believed and what she taught. Things were so bad that if a third person joined a conversation, she had to be careful because she didn't know who she could trust.

The Hungarians could not be honest about their feelings anymore because if you said the wrong things, you'd likely end up in jail. The school principal was a member of the Communist Party, but only on paper. There was no other way he could support his family except by taking part in a farce that he did not believe in. Anikó knew he was a very good man, and most of the teachers knew why he had to "play the part."

Other teachers, however, went along to get along. One was a churchgoing, Bible-thumping man who prayed all the time, but when the government changed leadership, he also changed his belief system. He taught that Lenin's teachings were the only way. He never opened his Bible again because of his career.

People were literally selling their souls to save their hides. Obviously, this man was not grounded soundly in his Christian faith, or he would have never buckled under the persecution of the Christians by the Communists.

Health Issues

In June 1956, Anikó fell dangerously ill. She had a form of rheumatoid arthritis, which affected all her joints and was extremely painful. She didn't realize that scurvy was still raging through her body

Miklós wanted to take his mother's temperature. The result was 40.2 degrees Celsius (104.7 Fahrenheit), but Miklós misread it and told his mom that it was 42 degrees Celsius (107.6 Fahrenheit). Miklós fell on his mother's chest and sobbed, "Mommy, you're going to die. What's to become of us?"

Anikó thought she should recheck the thermometer, which turned out to be a good idea. She tried to console her son that she would live and take care of him and his sister. Her temperature remained high, however, so she had to be hospitalized. Even then, doctors could not get her temperature down for three weeks.

While in the hospital, the doctors were looking for the cause of her illness. They found that the roots of six of her molars, which she lost when she was pregnant with Miklós, had become infected since she didn't get enough calcium in her diet while she was carrying him.

A special dentist had to be brought in to remove all six of her infected roots. They concluded that her symptoms were probably brought on by the serious infection in her mouth, which also affected her heart. Malnutrition, the stress of their situation, and total exhaustion finally took their toll on her body.

She stayed in the hospital for three months, where they had to teach her to walk all over again, and she left the hospital with a cane in August 1956. When the school year started in September, she could not resume teaching. She was still in too much pain and too weak to work.

Meanwhile, László worked odd jobs whenever he could, but their financial situation was becoming desperate. The main breadwinner was incapable of providing for her family. Anikó could not see any form of relief.

The future looked very bleak. Something had to change!

3

Different Strokes

Z oli's dream finally became a reality when he qualified for the Olympics.

At the age of seventeen, he swam for Hungary in the 1948 Summer Games, which took place in late July at the Empire Pool in London, England. He competed in the freestyle event, so the method of the stroke was not regulated like the backstroke, breaststroke, and butterfly events. Nearly all swimmers used the front crawl or a variant of that stroke.

Because the Olympic size swimming pool was fifty meters long, his race consisted of two lengths of the pool. Zoltán Szilárd placed third in the semifinals and seventh at the Olympics, which was a great achievement for Hungary. He became quite famous in his country. Everyone knew his name, and he loved every minute of his fame.

Zoli was very handsome, and the girls loved him. He married a beautiful model in 1954, and they had a child within one year. The marriage didn't last too long, however, because Zoli had different plans.

In August 1956, before the revolution in Hungary, Zoli and three of his swimming buddies decided they would escape to Austria and leave behind the country that was no longer free but controlled by the Communist regime. They got on a cruise ship on the Danube River, which ran north before making a sharp turn and running west along the border of Hungary, Czechoslovakia, and Austria. The ship had to make a U-turn and head back to Budapest when it got halfway through the cruise. They decided that they would jump overboard when the ship got as close as possible to Austria.

They paced back and forth on the ship, waiting for the right moment, and when the time came, Zoli yelled out, "Now! Let's go!" They all dived overboard and started swimming for shore. The patrol on the ship saw them, and they sent out small boats to capture them all. They started shooting at the swimmers. Zoli was so well trained in holding his breath that he swam under the swirling patrol boats for several minutes at a time.

Two of his buddies were shot and killed. The third was wounded and gave himself up, but at least he was alive. The river turned red with blood, and the shots from the patrol boats were deafening as Zoli tried to avoid getting hit. The people aboard the ship screamed in panic since they had no idea what was happening. Some thought a war had broken out. Zoli was the only one who managed to get away with just a small wound to his leg from the propeller of the patrol boat. He crawled to shore and hid in the bushes, where he fainted. He had made it to Austria.

When the revolution broke out in Hungary on October 23, 1956, Zoli returned to Hungary in November because he heard that several American diplomats were jailed in Hungary, and he wanted to help free them from prison. He was twenty-six years old, and because he was known as a hero in Hungary, he felt that he was indestructible. He successfully helped the Americans escape from jail and then assisted them in getting out of Hungary. Indeed, he succeeded in helping many more people flee the country. Zoli truly was a hero.

All of his life, Zoli was extremely brave—almost to the point of stupidity—and loved taking chances. He got a thrill from being on the edge of danger. Throughout his life, he had many episodes that could have been fatal to him and others, but he always managed to get through them without permanent damage. He and Anikó were total opposites of each other. He lived on the wild side, and Anikó was always the steady, safe, trustworthy one.

He wasn't as successful in his personal life, though. Zoli would marry six times and have five children, but he definitely lived a full life.

4

Crossing the Line

*O*n October 23, 1956, a peaceful student demonstration in Budapest produced a list of sixteen demands for reform and greater political freedom. As the students attempted to broadcast these demands, police made arrests and tried to disperse the crowd with tear gas. When the students attempted to free those arrested, the police opened fire on the crowd, setting off a chain of events that led to the Hungarian Revolution.

That night, commissioned officers and soldiers joined the students on the streets of Budapest. Stalin's statue was brought down, and the protesters chanted, "Russians go home."

On October 25, Soviet tanks opened fire on protesters in Parliament Square. The students used Molotov cocktails to fight the Russian tanks since they had no other weapons. One journalist at the scene, saw twelve dead bodies and estimated that 170 had been wounded.

Stalin's statue brought down during the Revolution in 1956

1956 Revolution, showing destruction in Budapest

Soviet Tanks in Budapest, November 1956

Before the revolution, on October 20, Imre Nagy announced that he was freeing Cardinal József Mindszenty and other political prisoners. He also informed the people that his government intended to abolish the one-party state. Nagy's most controversial decision took place on November 1, when he announced that Hungary intended to withdraw from the Warsaw Pact as well as proclaiming Hungarian neutrality. He also asked the United Nations to become involved in the country's dispute with the Soviet Union. Britain and France were involved in the Suez crisis in Egypt, and Eisenhower did not think Hungary was worth a world war, so he did not send American troops to help. When the United Nations suggested an investigation, Russia used its veto to stop it.

Nikita Khrushchev, the leader of the Soviet Union, became increasingly concerned about these developments. On November 4, 1956, he sent the Red Army into Hungary. Soviet tanks immediately captured Hungary's airfields, highway junctions, and bridges. Fighting took place all over the country, but the Hungarian forces were quickly defeated.

During the Hungarian Uprising, an estimated 20,000 people were killed, nearly all during the Soviet intervention. Imre Nagy was arrested and replaced by the Soviet loyalist, Miklós Kádár. Nagy was imprisoned until being executed in 1958.

Eleven years had passed since Anikó and László fled their country for a few months in 1945 because of the war. They were again faced with a decision to leave or stay under the horrific conditions since their country was fighting for freedom by revolting against the Russian oppression.

"I can't go on like this!" exclaimed Anikó. "We are so poor, and the future looks bleak. We have to get out of here!"

László proposed a solution. "I've heard thousands of people are escaping across the border to Austria. Do you think we should try?"

Anikó and László talked about it for several hours. They decided to ask their children, Zsuzsi, ten years old, and Miklós, eleven years old, for their opinion.

"Zsuzsi, what do you think about leaving Hungary and going far away to America?"

Zsuzsi, a timid little girl, replied, "I don't care. If you tell me we go, we go. If you tell me we stay, we stay."

They asked Miklós the same question, but his reply was different. He broke down in tears and said, "Please, let's go Mommy, because maybe in America I can have more than lard on bread for my lunch, and maybe even some salami or sausage on it. Plus, we probably won't have to stand in line for bread and pay with glass bottles because that really embarrasses me."

That was the deciding factor for Anikó. The impact of her son's plea made such a strong impression on her that when she and László were alone that night, she screamed, looking toward heaven, "If I have to die trying, I will get out of this cursed country and give my children a better life!"

Anikó found out that her best friend, Magda, and her family had already escaped since her husband was one of the young men fighting in the revolution and had to leave before Russians caught up with them. Hearing this also inspired Anikó and László to make their decision.

On December 6, 1956, Anikó walked into her principal's office at school, knowing that he was only a member of the Communist party on paper. She told him her situation, which he already knew, and pleaded with him to give her a transfer letter to a school near the Austrian border.

The principal knew exactly what she had in mind, and she was taking a big chance because he could have had her arrested and thrown in jail immediately. He walked up to her, gave her a big hug, and said, "I agree with your decision. I would love to go myself, but I have four young children, and I could not try escaping with all of them."

He gave her a transfer letter that would help them get on a train heading toward Austria. "May God bless you and keep you safe," he said. "Let me also give you the name of a man who lives right on the border of Hungary and Austria. Give him whatever money you have, and he'll help you cross over the border."

He handed Anikó a piece of paper with a name and address, then told her to go home.

On December 8, 1956, Anikó, László, Miklós, and Zsuzsi boarded a train heading for a town close to the border of Hungary and Austria. It was quite obvious what they were about to do since they had two suitcases with them and looked scared to death. There were others on the train who had the same plan since the borders were still open. The Russians had not laid down mines yet, so hundreds, if not thousands, were escaping daily. No one spoke because they were frozen with fear. They arrived in Sopron where they had to stay in a hotel overnight.

As they were checking in, they saw Russian soldiers coming toward the hotel to ask for identification and ask why people were staying there. They knew that anyone who would stay in a hotel close to the Austrian border would definitely want to escape, and they had to stop them.

Anikó, László, and the kids, frightened to death, started running up the stairs and hid in the attic so they would not be caught. They all huddled in a corner and told the kids not to make any noise. The Russian soldiers came up to the attic, but they did not see the family hiding, so they left.

With a big sigh of relief, László said, "Let's go to our room. Don't make a sound, and we'll be all right."

They spent the night in the hotel room, but didn't get much sleep that night. The next day, they got on a bus heading for the Austrian border, to the little town where they would get help. Russian soldiers stopped the bus within a half hour.

As the Russians stepped on the bus, one of the soldiers said in broken Hungarian, "Ve vant to see papers with stamp on it." They were looking for official paperwork that would prove that everyone was traveling legally.

"This is it, it's over!" László whispered to Anikó. "We have no official papers. They will kill us for sure now!"

Suddenly, he remembered Anikó's transfer letter that had a stamp on it. He reached into his pocket, pulled it out, and showed it to the Russian soldier. The Russian looked at the letter, turned it over, and seeing the stamp and the big letters on it, he said, "Good paper, you go." He didn't understand a word on the form, obviously, but he still let them continue on their journey. Anikó's heart dropped back down from her throat as the soldiers got off the bus, and she held her children close.

Within a few hours, they arrived at the border and looked up the man who was supposed to help them. He welcomed them and fed them some dinner. He advised them to wait until 1 a.m. to start walking since the border patrol would be lightly staffed at that time. Also, he knew one of the guards who would be on duty and would help them get started. Anikó gave the man one month's salary, which is all the money they had.

On December 10, 1956, at precisely one o'clock in the morning, they began their escape. Anikó, László, Miklós, Zsuzsi, and the guard started walking toward Austria. He walked with them about a mile before he set them off on their own.

The guard pointed west. "Just keep walking that way, and within a couple of miles you will be in Austria. The border is not marked or fenced, so you will not know when you have crossed over. Good luck!"

László was carrying two suitcases that contained everything they could bring. Anikó was walking with a cane, still unsteady from her illness. The type of arthritis she had was slow to heal, so she was still in a lot of pain as she walked.

"I hope I can make it. It hurts with every step I take," Anikó complained. Her need to get her family out of the country overcame any discomfort, and she endured every painful step.

"Don't worry, none of us can go any faster with all this snow on the ground slowing us down," replied László.

Rifle fire broke the silence.

"Oh, my God, what was that? It sounds like a machine gun!" Anikó stifled the urge to scream.

"Someone is shooting! Look over there," László whispered. "Do you see all those people dropping like flies?"

Anikó and the kids looked across the moonlit meadow, and saw people being executed. They were terrified and started walking faster, but they didn't run so they wouldn't call attention to themselves. Immediately, Anikó put Zsuzsi behind her and László put Miklós behind him. That way, if they were shot at, the bullets would strike the parents first.

Anikó was thinking they had made a mistake, taking this kind of chance. *What if our children get killed and we survive? How could we ever forgive ourselves?*

The meadow turned into a dense forest, so at least they were not out in the open any more. Zsuzsi, frozen with fear, had to go to the bathroom. Since they were outdoors, her mother took her aside and told her to pee in the bushes. As they walked some more, not knowing how much further they had to go, they saw someone coming toward them with a flashlight. He was getting closer and closer. They were all petrified, thinking it was a Russian soldier. László dropped both suitcases, sat on one, and started sobbing. He was sure they were caught.

As the light came closer, there were two figures. One of them spoke in Hungarian, saying, "Are you people all right? Who are you?"

When László saw that two Austrian border patrolmen had come to help them, he almost screamed with happiness! They were in Austria! They had escaped unharmed!

The patrolmen led them to a school where there were several hundred refugees. They received some food and a cot to sleep on. The next day, they were taken by a streetcar to a high school in Vienna that had been opened for refugees. The school was on top of a snow-covered hill with pine trees everywhere. While riding in the streetcar, an older lady noticed Zsuzsi. She got up from her seat and offered Zsuzsi a piece of chocolate. It was obvious to the woman that they were refugees since they spoke Hungarian. She wanted to show them some kindness.

Anikó saw it differently. She felt embarrassed that they had sunk so low that they were receiving handouts from strangers. She began weeping silently, but with hope in her heart, she felt that things could only get better.

Since it was December, everything was covered with snow—the most gorgeous sight this family had seen in a long time. As they arrived, the women and children were led into the gym, and the men were accommodated in the cafeteria. There were hundreds of Hungarian refugees already, but the Austrians made sure everyone had a place to sleep.

Canada and the United States were sponsoring the shelters, so the two countries sent clothing, toiletries, and other personal items. Anikó and Zsuzsi were excited to rummage through the clothing and find something decent to wear.

Zsuzsi yelled out, "Mommy, look at this beautiful warm coat. Do you think I can have it?"

"Yes, darling, you can keep it." As she picked out a few dresses for herself, she thought, *I already have more clothes than I've had in years!*

They stayed in this school for six weeks and spent Christmas with the other refugees. Everyone looked forward to a new life of freedom. During the Christmas holidays, an Austrian film studio came to make a movie about the refugees. All the children were asked to get up on the stage in the gym and sing Hungarian Christmas carols to a piano accompaniment.

Anikó noticed that the camera did not focus on Miklós and Zsuzsi at all. *What is wrong with this guy? Can't he tell that these two kids are the cutest?* Finally, they got so see the movie in a theater, and to Anikó's surprise, there was a close-up of Zsuzsi's face during one whole song. So Miklós and Zsuzsi were even movie stars now!

After leaving Hungary for the last time, Zoli searched the Austrian shelters and found Anikó and

László. He informed them that he had to catch a plane soon, and he would be going to America.

Anikó was confused when she heard this news. "Why are you able to fly to America when I just found out we have to take a ship and go to Canada?"

"Because I aided in rescuing two American diplomats from jail and helped them across the border," he replied. "They told me that I could have any reward I wanted. I decided I wanted to go to America—by plane."

"Oh, you're the big shot of the family," Anikó said, teasing her brother. "Good luck. We'll call you when we get to Canada."

It would be months before that phone call was made.

5

A New Chapter, a New World

*T*he Canadian government sent officials to Austria to organize travel for the refugees. They could only take a couple hundred people at a time, so Anikó and her family didn't leave the high school until the end of January.

The family was put on a train and transported to the port city of Bremerhaven, West Germany, where they boarded a huge ship called *Berlin*. They were given their own cabin, which gave them some privacy for a change. Then the ship left the dock for a nine-day voyage across the Atlantic Ocean.

Berlin ship that takes Anikó and her family to Canada, 1957

Zsuzsi with her 'new coat', Anikó and Miklós on Berlin ship

The first day was great. They all stood out on the deck and watched the coastline disappear in the distance. The following days were not as pleasant, however. Anikó, László, and Zsuzsi were terribly seasick, so they mainly stayed in the cabin and were unable to eat much. Miklós, on the other hand, didn't get seasick at all, so he stayed in the dining room and gorged himself with the most wonderful meals he had ever eaten. He had never had such delicious food—or so much of it!

"I can't even think of food," Zsuzsi moaned when her brother would describe his feasts. "Finally, we have all these delicious free meals, and I can't even look at them!"

"I know, sweetheart," Anikó consoled her. "It's not fair, but soon you'll be able to eat anything you want."

On the ninth day, they were getting close to the shoreline. The seasickness had abated. They all stood outside on the deck watching Halifax, Canada, getting closer and closer. Their hearts were pounding, and they were all thinking the same thing. *What is waiting for us? What will happen to us? What will this new world be like?*

As they got off the ship, they all had to be checked for transmittable diseases. After they gave Anikó a tuberculosis test, a doctor spoke to her, through a translator, saying, "Madame, you are not allowed to come to Canada. You have tuberculosis."

Anikó was petrified with fear and yelled out, "Now what will happen? Why can't we get a break? What will happen to my family?"

They were informed that she could go to a sanitarium, where doctors would try to cure her. Anikó underwent additional tests and discovered that she did not have TB, but was a carrier and could not infect anyone else.

After all the paperwork was completed, the officials noted that Anikó's name translated to Ann and László translated to Leslie. Zsuzsi became Susan, and Miklós translated to Nick. They had to go by their new names in Canada from that day forward.

They were put on a train and were allowed to get off at any city they wanted.

The immigrant family really enjoyed the train ride across the width of Canada. They were given their own sleeping room, but most days they would stare out the plate-glass windows to see what this new country was like. They saw beautiful homes and gardens, but one thing really amazed them—most people had TVs in their homes!

"These people must be really rich because almost every house has a television," observed Nick. None of them had ever seen one before. They had only heard of them, so they were quite fascinated.

One of the conductors on the train was a black man. As he walked through the coaches, Ann whispered to Leslie, "I have only heard about black people. This is the first one I have ever seen! How interesting!"

Nick and Susan could not take their eyes off of him either, although they knew it was rude to stare. Anikó asked the conductor, through an interpreter, if it would be all right to have their picture taken with him. He had no idea what this was all about, but he agreed.

Winnipeg, in the province of Manitoba, was the only city where they could get help. They would be allowed to stay at the Hungarian Immigration Office for a year until they could get on their feet. They had heard that Ann's best friend was living in Winnipeg, so that was the best choice.

Within three days, they arrived in Winnipeg and were taken to the Hungarian Immigration building, where they were given a small room with bunk beds. They were shown the lunchroom, the community bathrooms, and a community room where they could get together with other immigrants. The first few days were spent filling out forms, so they could be official residents.

Since neither Ann nor Leslie spoke English, they welcomed the idea of having some support until they could get jobs. They realized they would have to find work that required minimal language skills. Ann could not teach, and Leslie could not write for a newspaper because they spoke no English.

Different churches were sending people to the Immigration Office to find a family that they could sponsor. Ann's friend, Magda, came a few days later with a couple from the Anglican Church who had helped her and her family out when they arrived. These people offered Ann and Leslie the opportunity to live in their home for six weeks since they would be traveling to Europe. The couple came to get the family the next day and took them to their house, so they could show them around.

Ann wanted to know where they kept the key to the house, but she didn't know any English. She pointed at the lock on the front door and shrugged her shoulders. The lady of the house smiled when she realized that Ann wanted to know how to lock the door. She showed with her fingers, "No key, no key." That's when Ann understood that they *didn't* lock their doors.

"Wow!" Leslie exclaimed. "Now that's something unheard of in our country. What a difference between this country and ours."

Before they left on their long trip, the family also found jobs for Ann and Leslie. Ann started working as a cleaning lady in a nursing home for 49 cents an hour. Leslie got a job with a printing company for 75 cents per hour. They didn't have to speak very much English for these jobs, which made it possible to be employed.

Moving In

After being gone six weeks, the host family returned home. Within a few days, they had all of their church friends over to welcome the refugee family from Hungary. They brought household goods, including a set of china, silverware, pots and pans, linens, towels, and lamps—just about every-thing they needed to set up house. The generous couple also found them an apartment, paid the first three months' rent, and moved them in the next day. On the day of the move, a flow of people from the Anglican Church arrived non-stop, bringing sofas, a dining table, chairs, beds, and dressers. By nightfall, the family had a fully furnished apartment.

Ann and Leslie could not believe their eyes.

All they could do was stare in amazement at the stream of people coming with different household items. They kept repeating the only English words they knew— "Thank you, thank you!"

Leslie and Ann had become "rich" all of a sudden. They had a warm, fully furnished home with indoor plumbing. The beds were made, the lamps were lit, the kitchen cupboards were stocked, and the refriger-ator was full of food. Now they could eat meat every day if they wanted to.

"I think we made the right decision escaping from Hungary," beamed Leslie as he looked around their apartment.

With a beautiful smile on her face, Ann teared up. She *knew* that they had made the right decision.

6

On Their Own at Last

*A*nn cooked every day, and whipping up meals in the kitchen was enjoyable. She didn't have to get creative because they had meat, butter, and flour. Best of all, they actually could afford bananas and oranges, which was quite a treat for them since they never got to eat these things back in Hungary.

Nick and Susan were put into school immediately, but since they did not speak English, the nuns at Holy Ghost School put them back two grades. They were asked to sit in the back of the room along with a couple of German kids who were also learning English.

Their job was to sit and listen. It took Nick and Susan several months before they could understand anything. They had no problem with math, however, which they both excelled in. Ann and Leslie enrolled in an evening school to learn English, which they attended twice a week. It was more difficult for them to learn the language than the children since they were older and young children pick up languages more easily.

When Ann went to work, she sometimes held an electric floor polisher in one hand and Hungarian/English flash cards in the other. The nursing home was run by a Catholic ministry, and a nun would occasionally check Ann's work.

"Once in a while, why don't you move that machine over a little bit. It's getting quite shiny in that one spot!" the nun said as she tried to show Ann by moving the machine a few inches. Then she would smile and walk away.

One day, an old lady in the home was pointing under her bed to show Ann that she had her shoes underneath and could not reach them. Ann immediately got on her knees and pulled out the lady's shoes. The old lady was so grateful that she gave Ann a 25-cent tip.

Ann saw it as a handout and started crying. *Is this what I have come to? Do I always have to be the pauper?*

Ann swallowed her pride when she realized that she had to work a half-hour to get that much money. *I need to stop pitying myself and just say thank you.* She had to get used to this new country and what was acceptable. Their etiquette here was quite different from what she was accustomed to.

A nun offered her grapes one day, but keeping with the Hungarian custom, she declined. She hoped the nun would offer again, but she didn't. In Hungary, it was polite to decline the first time, so as not to appear too anxious. Things were different here.

She would have loved to have some grapes, so after that incident, if anyone offered her something free, she took the first offer. Her whole family realized that this was definitely a different country and culture, and people wanted to do nice things for others without expecting anything in return.

Everything was new and exciting, so it didn't take long before they started to really appreciate their amazing life. They learned to be content with what they had and not whine about what they didn't have.

The feelings of desperation and resentment, caused by the living conditions in Hungary, were replaced with gratitude when they realized that the Canadian government and local citizens had taken them in, helped them, and given them an opportunity to better themselves. People who have never experienced poverty cannot truly appreciate how fortunate they really are.

Since both Ann and Leslie were born into wealthy families, it was even more difficult for them to live at the poverty level. It was amazing to them that they had endured a life of despair in Hungary for eleven years. Nick and Susan, on the other hand, had only known poverty all their lives, so this privileged life was new to them. They appreciated every minute in Canada.

During recess at school one day, a couple of the kids were playing catch with an orange. One of the kids overthrew, and the orange hit a wall and exploded. Nick and Susan were angry, remembering the orange they had received as a Christmas present one year back in Hungary. They could still remember the taste of that sweet, juicy gift. Here in Canada, there was nothing they could do about this "crime" because they didn't speak much English. They realized that these kids did not appreciate what they had since they had never experienced anything different.

There was only one thing that was difficult to get used to—the cold weather. Winnipeg, Manitoba, had severe winter conditions where the temperature could drop to 50 below zero with the wind chill factor. Although it snowed in Hungary, the snow didn't stay on the ground more than a couple of months, and winters never got *this* cold.

In Winnipeg, however, the winter lasted seven to nine months. It wasn't unusual to see snow on the ground for up to six months. Spring came and went quickly, followed by six short weeks of summer. Although these seasons were fleeting, their beauty made up for it.

The locals joked about summer in Winnipeg. They said it arrived every August 5th and lasted between 1 p.m. and 4 p.m. As for fall, this season brought a breathtaking display of red and golden leaves on the tree-lined streets.

Learning English Well

One afternoon, Ann came home from work and heard children's voices singing in Hungarian. She heard laughter, and it sounded like the children were having a great time. Ann was surprised to discover that Nick and Susan were teaching their new neighbor friends Hungarian songs.

Ann chuckled to herself. *This is not the way it's supposed to happen. My kids should be learning English, not teaching other kids Hungarian songs!*

As it turned out, there was no reason to worry. Her kids were speaking fluent English within one year. Ann and Leslie, however, were struggling with spelling and how to use the past, present, and future tenses correctly. It wasn't as easy for them as for the kids.

Leslie worked hard at the printing company. Since he had natural talent, the manager decided to train him in a specialized procedure known as "offset stripping." This consisted of working with negatives, then developing the pictures in a dark room and transferring the images onto an aluminum sheet, which the printer would use to make prints. If it was a color image, four different metal sheets would have to be made—yellow, cyan, magenta, and black. They were printed on top of each other to achieve the right color.

Leslie picked this technique up quickly and received one raise after another. Besides the printing job, he also started writing bulletins for the Hungarian Catholic Church in Winnipeg.

On the home front, Ann gave her children 25 cents per week for an allowance so they could learn the value of the money. Nick and Susan were both very good at budgeting their money, and they did not spend this modest allowance foolishly.

When their first Christmas in Canada finally arrived, they were able to afford a small Christmas tree. Ann began thinking about the time the neighbor girl in Hungary showed off her new doll to Susan and decided to make up for this humiliation. She bought Susan the most beautiful doll she could afford, and for Nick, she chose a BB gun that he had always wanted.

1st Christmas in Canada, Susan's new doll

Nick at 12 with BB gun

Susan had saved some of her allowance so she gave her mother and father a small plastic angel holding a star that could be used as an ornament. The trinket cost Susan more than one week of allowance, a whole 39 cents. Nick was taking a woodcraft class in school at the time. He made a small magazine rack with a tabletop, which he gave to his parents for Christmas.

Ann and Leslie both worked hard, and by 1958 they were able to afford their first car, a 1939 Pontiac. Leslie had been taking driving lessons, so when it was time to purchase the car, he could hardly wait to get behind the wheel of his very first vehicle.

"Check this out! Is this the most beautiful car you have ever seen?" Leslie boasted as he pulled into the driveway. "You'll have to learn how to drive soon, Ann, so you can experience this. Come on kids, let's go for a ride. You'll love this!"

They all piled into their "new" car, and Leslie drove off, proud as a peacock that they could finally afford such a nice vehicle. They drove around for hours, going nowhere in particular. Nick and Susan were now twelve and thirteen, and they were not used to luxuries like this, that most people took for granted.

In 1959, Zoli came to visit them from California, driving a new convertible. "Come on, Sis. I'll teach you how to drive a real car! If you learned to drive that huge Pontiac, you can drive a tank. But let's start with my convertible first."

They took many long rides in his convertible, but Zoli was doing most of the driving. Since they had not seen each other in several years, Ann inquired about his life.

"When I first arrived in Long Beach, I was offered a machinist position at Bethlehem Steel," he began. "I didn't need to speak the language, but I had some experience working with lathes." A lathe is a machine that spins a block of material to perform various operations such as cutting, sanding, or drilling. The secret to successfully operating a lathe is to keep the cutting tools sharp by using a slip stone across the top surface. Then the sides rarely need attention. The knowledge that Zoli had gained in Hungary served him well in America.

"One morning, I was given a rush job. I had to adjust a tool, and in my hurry to get the job done, I didn't fasten it correctly. When I turned the machine on, this tool flew off, spinning out of control, and smashed against my groin. I cursed in Hungarian, and the workmen around me knew there was something wrong. I crashed to the floor in agonizing pain, while grabbing between my legs. There was blood gushing out of my pants, and when the supervisor saw how serious this was, he called an ambulance.

"After I arrived at the hospital, I got cleaned up and examined by the doctors. They concluded that my penis and one of my testicles had been severed pretty badly. They immediately went to work, and after major pain medication and anesthesia, they sewed up the wound and tried to make me as comfortable as possible."

Ann listened, transfixed. But there was more to the story.

"A few days later, I started worrying that maybe my injuries had caused me to become impotent. I was feeling sorry for myself. After all, I was only in my thirties, and quite a handsome man, even if I say so myself. I loved the ladies and had quite an appetite for the opposite sex."

"I thought that I could not go on with life if my manhood was compromised. I feared I would never experience the joy of making love again. I didn't know what would become of me. I became extremely depressed and didn't want to eat or speak to anyone. It was a challenge just to urinate, so I didn't want to drink anything either.

"A few days later, a fairly attractive nurse came into my room and told me she was there to give me a sponge bath. When she started to wash my private area, she tried to be as gentle as she could, but being touched down there started to get the blood flowing. That's when I realized that my manhood was still intact. I yelled at the nurse, 'Get out! Get out of here!' I closed my eyes, so I wouldn't have to look at her because the pain was unbearable. I was sure that most of my stitches would burst."

Ann thought she might bust out laughing, but she kept a serious face as her brother continued his story.

"My whole attitude changed after that. I ate, drank, and did whatever I was told so I could get out of the hospital and get well again. I was happy beyond belief to realize that I would be able to have a normal sex life again."

Driving Around

Ann was so enthralled with his story that she forgot that she was supposed to be getting a driving lesson. They both laughed at the embarrassing situation he had been in. She actually was not surprised since she remembered her brother always getting into some kind of predicament. She finally said, "All right, let's concentrate on my driving lesson now!"

She was a good student and mastered the basics after a few lessons. She had been excited beyond belief to get her driver's license. She passed the test on her first attempt and was thrilled that she would be able to drive her children to school and run errands.

Camping became a favorite weekend activity after they could finally afford a tent. They usually went camping with friends, so the families would spend a lot of time together. Leslie was not very social, however. He usually just sat on a chair and read books or magazines, while Ann and the kids played cards, went swimming or boating, or just relaxed.

They started going to a Hungarian Catholic Church together as a family. Ann and Leslie felt it was important to introduce Christianity to their children since they had not been able to do that in Hungary. Ann and Leslie were confident that their kids would be able to make their own decisions about God when they were older.

Now that her children were getting a religious education, Ann was even more appreciative of Canada's "blue laws." All stores were closed on Sundays.

Many day-to-day activities were not allowed. Sunday was a day to spend with family, worshipping God.

7

Trying to Make a Living

*A*nn struggled to keep a job long term. She left the nursing home within a year and went to work in a paint factory so she could be around younger people. She was required to pour paint into metal containers, and the stench of the paint made her sick. She often became impaired to the point that she could not perform her job properly. In 1958, there were no quality controls on lead or chemicals in paint. She only worked at this job for three months because of the dangerous fumes.

Ann got another job working in an egg factory. She had to break 8,000 eggs in one day and seperate the yolks and whites in containers. She did not have to speak English for this job, and at 80 cents per hour, she was willing to give it a try. Unfortunately, the eggs were very cold, and her hands ached by the end of the day.

There were several men working there who brought the women 200 eggs at a time. One particular man would always bring Ann her eggs, and every time he laid the carton down, he touched Ann's hand or arm. She didn't care for this at all, but she let it go for a couple of months. Then, the unforgivable happened. One morning when he brought her the eggs, he grabbed one of her breasts. She was thirty-two at the time, and this man was about fifty-five—an *old* man in her estimation.

Okay, now that's enough!

She went to the manager, but since she still couldn't speak English too well, she pointed at the man and then pointed at her breast. As she was trying to explain what had happened, the man who touched her threw an egg at her back. The egg broke, and she felt the gooey mess soaking her shirt.

She started crying. "No work, me no work!"

Her manager tried to console her and told her to get back to work. The attacker gave her a dirty look and slammed the rest of his eggs down. Then he cursed under his breath and stormed out the door.

A few weeks later, he came into the room where Ann was working, and she knew that he was looking for her. Her heart started pounding as he spotted her and began walking across the room. She thought she might faint if he got any closer. Scared to death, she started backing away from him when he asked in Hungarian, "Are you Ann?"

Stunned, Ann replied in Hungarian, "Yes."

His face was kind now. He begged her, "Please forgive me for what I did to you. I do it with all the ladies here, and they don't seem to mind. It's all in good fun, just to pass the day faster. You are the first person who complained about it. Please forgive me."

Ann could see that he was sincere in his apology. "Fine, just don't let it happen again."

They spoke for several minutes and soon became friends. At break time, they talked about their families and adventures they had experienced. Ann worked at the egg factory for six months. During that time, she often thought about the difficulties she had faced in Hungary. Back in the old country, she had to stand in line for one egg, while in Canada, she was breaking 8,000 eggs in *one day*. What a difference in the two countries! Now when she baked, if the recipe called for six eggs, she always put in eight, just because she could.

Ann remained close with her dear friend Magda, who was employed with a macaroni factory. Magda encouraged Ann to apply for a position that would pay $1.10 per hour. Once again, Ann quit her job— the third time in two years—and went to work at the Creamette Macaroni Factory. She worked there from 1958 to 1962, but the laborious strain took its toll on her body.

Her job was to lift heavy stacks of ten boxes off a conveyer belt and pack them in larger boxes. The conveyer belt moved very quickly, so she tried not to make a mistake. She had to be careful and pay attention so the boxes would not topple off the stacks, yet work at a pace fast enough to keep up with the conveyer belt. Most of the time, she felt like she could barely keep up.

She tried hard to lift the boxes correctly, but many of them still ended up on the floor. Her arms were throbbing by the end of the day, but at least she was getting a good workout.

Ann continued to struggle, so the forelady spent some time training her. She demonstrated the proper procedure, then she would let Ann try.

Ann made several attempts to lift the boxes correctly during the first training session, but they still flew up in the air and crashed on the floor.

Each time they fell, the forelady said, "Oh, shit."

After hearing "Oh, shit" repeated over and over, Ann went home and told Leslie, "Get the dictionary. I learned a new word today."

"How do you spell it?" he asked.

"I don't know, but it starts with the letter O. My supervisor kept saying *oshet, oshet*."

Obviously, Leslie could not find the word under the O's in the dictionary. Many years later when they found out what the two words were, they rolled with laughter and kept telling the story over and over again to their friends. Ann finally got the hang of picking up a stack of ten boxes at a time, and within a few weeks, she wasn't dropping them anymore. Her arms were not sore either, and she was getting shapely biceps.

During the summer when Susan turned thirteen, Ann taught her how to cook. Ann would gather the ingredients the night before, and in the morning, she would leave Susan instructions about how to cook the meal.

By the time Ann came home at 5 p.m., Susan had the table set and prepared a wonderful home-cooked meal that was waiting for the family. Ann, Susan, and

Nick ate dinner together every night. Leslie was not able to join them, however, because his work scheduled changed constantly. Some nights, he would come home as late as 11 p.m. His excuse was usually that there was just too much to do at work.

The four of them ate together only on Sundays after the church service. Leslie never could find any time to spend with his children, and this really started to bother Ann.

She would eventually learn the truth about why he was never home in the evenings.

8

Dreams Come True

*L*eslie's dream was to build his own home, using architectural plans that he had designed. To help make this dream come true, Ann got a second job working the night shift in a lab, cleaning test tubes. The test tubes were caked with dried blood as well as many other unidentifiable substances. She had to soak the test tubes in soapy water and clean each one with a bottle brush.

Ann realized after she took the job that this was a big mistake because her children were teenagers, and she should be home keeping an eye on them. She took Susan with her to help out, so she could at least be sure that her daughter wasn't getting into any trouble. She and Susan could have gotten some very serious illnesses working in the lab, but she believed that God protected them.

When they had saved up enough money so that Leslie could open his own printing shop, Ann started working with him. He really enjoyed being his own boss, especially since he could come and go as he pleased, which he did.

In 1962, Leslie's dream started to become a reality. They bought a piece of property and started the construction of their new three-bedroom house. Ann just could not believe this was happening. "Think about it, Leslie. Five short years ago, we were refugees without a dime to our name, and look at us now! Hard work really pays off."

They compared their success in Canada to their desperate situation in Hungary. There was no way they could have ever achieved what they had now if they had stayed. In Canada, a little bit of hard work went a long way. Capitalism worked. When people were given a chance to make it on their own, effort paid off.

Everything does have a price though, and Ann was paying. She didn't realize that she had become a robot. She went to work, came home to eat, went to another job, and did not spend quality time with her kids, all for the sake of "things."

Was it worth it? She asked herself this question over and over.

She wanted to give her children the best of everything, but she didn't realize that the very best thing she could have given them was herself. She still couldn't do what she wanted, which was to stay home and be a housewife. Having a new house meant there were a lot of bills that had to be paid.

Ann and Leslie had gotten caught up in the Canadian version of the "American Dream." They tried to "keep up with the Joneses" as their social life picked up and they started hosting parties. There were several Hungarian families they liked to socialize with, but most of their friends were Canadian.

After living in Canada for five years, the whole family studied for the citizenship test and became Canadian citizens. They were proud to be "official."

Nick and Susan were teenagers with a lot of freedom. Since both of their parents were either working or socializing, they were free to do whatever they wanted. They both had the typical "teenage attitude," especially Susan.

She knew everything and did not want to be told otherwise. Ann had a hard time adjusting to this new person. It was difficult for her to realize that her children were growing up and had ideas of their own and wanted to express them. She couldn't understand why Susan would talk back at times and get a sassy tone in her voice.

Many years later, when Susan was a mother herself, she shared with Ann about the way she and Nick were treated as young teenagers and tried to explain why she had such a bad attitude sometimes. She told her mother that as a teenager, she felt like her feelings and opinions didn't count. Susan also shared her memories of her and Nick often being told by their father, "Go away. You are just a stupid child, and you don't know anything."

This left a permanent scar on Susan's heart, and it took her many years to get her self-esteem back because she never felt that she was good enough.

* * *

Magda's daughter, Maria, and Susan had become very good friends by the time they were about sixteen. They started hanging out with other teenagers at the CYO (Catholic Youth Organization). They enjoyed the dances, parties, outings, summer camps, and social gatherings. It was a special time for the girls to have some teenage experiences.

Some of the activities the girls were interested in did not please their parents. They started wearing lots of makeup and tight skirts. Maria was talented in applying makeup and creating hairstyles, and she and Susan would spend hours giving each other "makeovers." Ann and Leslie were quite concerned about the way Susan looked at times, and her father would tell her she looked like a call girl.

Her parents came of age in Hungary in the 1930s and '40s, when nice girls didn't wear makeup. In fact, Ann didn't put lipstick on for the first time until she was thirty-two years old.

But times had changed. Their family was living in Canada, and this was the Sixties, the hippie and free-love decade. Susan constantly reminded her parents, "You just don't understand! This is a different world!"

In spite of her looks and attitude, she still continued to cook in the summers when she was out of school. They had just moved into their brand new house a few months earlier, and Susan was preparing dinner. She put a skillet with cooking oil on the stove and turned on the heat. She was chopping the onion when the phone rang.

Susan ran to answer the phone. "Hello? Oh, hi, Johnny. How are you doing? I've been waiting for your call."

"Sorry, I have been busy, but I really would like to see you. When can we meet?"

Susan was so excited that Johnny wanted to see her that she chattered for fifteen minutes—until she saw smoke bellowing out of the kitchen.

She yelled in the phone, "Sorry, I have to go. There's smoke coming out of the kitchen. I think it's on fire!"

She slammed the phone down and ran into the kitchen. She saw high flames coming out of the skillet, already burning a corner of the cabinet. She had no idea what to do, so she picked up the skillet and put it on the floor, which was brand new linoleum. She managed to put out the flames on the cabinet, then grabbed the lid to the skillet and slammed it on top. She was lucky the house robe she was wearing hadn't caught on fire.

As soon as the fire was put out, she had a terrible feeling about where she had placed the skillet. Sure enough, there was a black melted hole in the linoleum.

Two thoughts ran through her head: *Should I kill myself, or should I run off to Alaska? If I stay, my father will kill me for sure.*

There was a third option—tell her parents. She called her mother at the print shop and told her what happened, crying and apologizing for burning a hole in the new floor. To her surprise, the only thing her mother said was, "Are you all right? You could have been badly burned! Who cares about that stupid floor!"

That night when her parents came home, the first thing they did was give her a big hug, and then they told her not to worry. The floor could be repaired. They were just relieved that she had not been hurt.

Unlike his sister, Nick was the more serious one, and he spent a lot of time in the basement creating and building gadgets. He enjoyed going out on dates and always had a girlfriend, but he wasn't interested in going to parties. He would rather stay home and tinker with his inventions.

In 1963 and 1964, Nick was president of his high school class and president of the Science Club at Dakota Collegiate in Winnipeg, Canada. He built many three-stage rockets that either included a small camera or live animals for experimentation. The camera had a single frame of 16mm film to snap one picture looking down from the trajectory's apogee (the point in the path when it reached the greatest height).

During one experiment, a hamster was sent up and returned with a parachute, but the animal was pronounced dead on arrival. The force of acceleration killed him during the launch sequence.

Another project, designed by Nick, was the construction of a meteorological station that was intended to be launched with a weather balloon. A balloon large enough was too expensive, however, so the unit was mounted on the bottom of a small airplane and flown once to test the instrumentation.

The meteorological station was mounted on an aluminum platform, and a clear plastic dome covered the assembly. It included a hygrometer, thermometer, barometer, and a precipitation sensor. Every instrument had an analog output, and the converted audio signal was recorded on a small reel-to-reel tape recorder. A modified 35mm camera took pictures vertically at the ground, and the data measurements were synchronized with the photographs.

The test was successful, and the project won an award at the annual school science fair. The project was later sent to Switzerland for an international competition. Not bad for an eighteen year old kid. His parents were proud of him!

Susan started showing interest in painting, so in the evenings she would join Nick downstairs and paint or sketch. Her parents always encouraged her and suggested she take art seriously since she showed so much talent. Later in life, painting would become one of her passions, and she would receive many awards for her art.

Nick and Susan were very close friends. Even though they fought with each other, when it came to protecting his little sister, Nick took things seriously. On extremely cold winter nights, Susan took the bus to get home and had to walk about fifteen minutes from the bus stop. Nick paced back and forth, checking outside, and with concern in his voice, he would say, "Where is she? She should have been home by now! We should go and try to find her."

Hearing Nick say this warmed Ann's heart. She was happy that her children loved each other as much as she loved *them*. Nick and Susan came home after school in the winter months and turned on the hose for several hours to flood their large backyard, which was ringed with pine trees. They did this for a couple of weeks, and finally they had a skating rink in their own backyard. Every day after school, they put on their ice skates and skated for hours.

By 1963, Ann and Leslie were able to afford a brand-new vehicle. They purchased a 1963 Chevrolet right off the showroom floor. They turned in their old car and applied for credit, which they were approved for immediately.

Finally, for the first time in their lives, Ann and Leslie had a new car—and credit. They were so happy! They spoke English well now, had a new house, their own business, a new car, and two wonderful teenagers. As far as Ann was concerned, life couldn't get any better than this.

Ann had been dreaming about a perfect life for many years. They had survived all those terrible years in Hungary, including two wars, and had started their lives over in a new country. They had worked hard to achieve everything they had. Finally, for the first time in decades, she was truly happy.

Ann had heard a saying many years ago that helped sustain her through her trials: *Yesterday's suffering is eased by the hope of tomorrow*. This was so true, and the hope of a new life, which she was now living, had truly eased her suffering.

One car wasn't enough, now that they were moving up in the world, so they purchased a second car. Ann drove the new Renault, and she took Nick out several times a week to teach him how to drive. Susan sat in the back seat, observing and looking forward to the day she would learn to drive. Their lessons were more challenging in the middle of winter, when everything was covered in ice and snow.

After a few lessons, Nick thought he knew how to drive, and as they were practicing, he would gaze up at the sky and talk about the airplanes instead of paying attention to what he was doing. When Ann saw this happening, she reprimanded her son. "You are not only responsible for your own life, but the lives of others. If I ever catch you taking your eyes off the road again, you can forget driving," she said.

After several more lessons, it was time for Nick to take his driver's test. He failed the first time because he tried to be cool and didn't pay attention to the speed limit. Ann was quite happy that he failed because maybe now he would pay attention. He passed the second time, so he was able to drive to school when his mother didn't need the car. He and Susan drove to school together, so Ann could stop worrying about them taking the bus.

Tragic News from Dallas

Zoli was still living in California, and he kept calling Ann with the same question, "When are you going to leave that horrible cold weather and move to Southern California, where our weather is beautiful most of the time?"

Ann's reply was always the same: "We are finally settled in our new home. The kids have their friends here, and we are very comfortable. We're not even thinking about moving. But you never know what the future will bring. That much I've learned in life."

Susan had started working part time for her father at his print shop. Ann, Leslie, and Susan were all together on Friday, November 22, 1963, when a special report interrupted the regular programming on the radio. A newsman with a trembling voice announced, "The President of the United States has been shot in Dallas, Texas. He's been rushed to the nearest hospital."

Susan yelled to her father, "Did you hear that? President Kennedy has just been shot!"

Leslie had not been paying attention to the radio, but now he and Ann rushed over to hear more of the tragic news. After several hours of broadcasting details of the shooting, the radio newsman announced that President Kennedy was dead on arrival at the hospital, but the First Lady, Jacqueline Kennedy, was unharmed.

Ann, Leslie, and Susan sat in silence while they tried to absorb what had just happened. Never in a million years did they think that a tragedy like this could happen in the United States. They had left a country where there was nothing but violence, only to come to North America and realize that tragedy happens everywhere. They were actually considering moving to the U.S., but after this horrific news, they thought they would wait a while.

They didn't wait too long, however.

9

And Dreams Can Shatter

One Saturday, Ann had to go into town to run some errands. It was late in the afternoon, about 3 p.m. As she was passing by the movie theater, she saw people exiting the matinee.

For a moment, she thought she was seeing things, but her husband was indeed one of the people coming out of the theater.

That morning, like most Saturdays, he had told Ann he had to work because there was so much business to take care of. Ann never questioned his whereabouts and always felt sorry for him since he always put in so many hours at the print shop.

When she saw her husband leaving the movie theater, she was determined to find the reason for his actions. She told herself that there was nothing wrong with him going to the movies. *But why did he have to lie about it? What was really happening?*

Ann also had a lot of business to take care of on Saturdays. Housecleaning, shopping, laundry, and errands took up most of the day. If she got everything done though, she and the family would have a free day on Sunday, and that was the goal.

Sundays were the only day the family spent together. They went to church, and afterwards, Leslie would have dinner with his family this one day of the week. After seeing him leave the movie theater, Ann realized that things could be different. He obviously did not *want* to spend more time with them. He had been lying all along, and this really wounded her.

She decided to wait and see how things would develop.

Several Saturdays later, Ann asked Nick to drive her into town in the Renault. They passed by the central park next to a motel. Ann was looking out the window and spotted a Chevrolet in the parking lot of the motel—*their* Chevrolet.

She didn't say anything to Nick, who hadn't noticed the car. Suddenly, she asked him to pull over to the side of the road. "Nick, drive the Renault home. I'll wait for your dad to pick me up in the other car."

Nick, totally unaware what was happening, was happy that he got to drive all the way home by himself.

After Nick left, Ann approached the car. Upon closer inspection, her heart sank when she confirmed that this was their vehicle. The car wasn't locked, so she got in and waited.

Over an hour had gone by when she saw her husband coming out of a motel room. As he approached the car, he saw Ann—and his face turned white as snow.

"Where were you?" asked Ann.

"I took a walk in the park," Leslie lied.

She knew that he had never taken a walk in his life. If he was getting any exercise, it was happening in the motel room.

"Then why were you coming out of that motel room?" Ann was getting angry.

"I don't know what you're talking about."

She did not question him anymore, but she realized that she was not only married to a liar, but her husband was also a cheater. This news totally devastated her, and she knew she could never trust him again. The love that she had always felt for him was suddenly gone.

Leslie, the person she had loved and trusted for eighteen years, had betrayed her, and there was no way their marriage would ever be the same again. She did not tell her children about what she saw that day, but they knew there was something wrong, just by watching the way their parents interacted with one another. Meanwhile, Ann suffered in silence and wondered why he would do something like that and hurt her so terribly.

During the long nights, she would lay awake, thinking well into the wee hours. *After all the terrible, trying times that we have been through together, after all the pain and sorrow that we have shared, why would he do this to me now when there is finally a light at the end of the tunnel?*

I worked my ass off at two jobs, earned pennies an hour, broke my back, and ignored my children just to get us somewhere, and this is the thanks I get?

I can't believe how many times he used work as an excuse for coming home late and for missing time with his children on Saturdays, when he was really out fooling around with other women. What kind of miserable, cruel, sadistic person would do that? He can't possibly love me. He's been using me all these years.

She started remembering times back in Hungary when Leslie would come home late at night because he was "looking for work." *Could he have been doing this even when I was the main one supporting the family? What should I do? Leave him or stay and stick it out, for better or for worse?*

This was definitely worse than all the other tragedies she had been through, but Ann decided to stay with him, and only heaven knows why. She had learned from her Christian education that once you get married, you stay married for the rest of your life. In her mind, divorce was not an option.

She didn't know that divorce was acceptable, according to the Bible, under certain circumstances—such as having an unfaithful husband. Since she didn't have time to read the Bible, she had no idea what God's Word said. Throughout the years, she had never attended a Bible study group since she had been too busy taking care of her family.

In Hungary, you were expected to stay with your spouse, no matter how miserable you were, so she felt obligated to keep with tradition. Of course, another reason she stayed with Leslie was for the sake of her children. She decided that she would just have to continue her marriage with a broken heart while

Leslie lived his life, not caring what she thought, doing exactly what he wanted.

Meanwhile, Ann's mother, Erzsébet Szilárd, who was now widowed, was waiting for paperwork that would allow her to leave Hungary and live close to her daughter. A couple of years earlier, Ann and Leslie had started the process to bring her to Canada. When the travel documents arrived, Erzsébet was on the next plane for Winnipeg. When Ann greeted her mother at the airport, she grabbed her like a little child would and sobbed in her mother's arms. "I've missed you so much!" Ann cried out. "It has been too many years since we have seen each other. Welcome to Canada!"

Ann was thrilled to have her mother living with them, especially because Erzsébet was a great help around the house. She was a wonderful cook, loved to play cards and had a warm, giving spirit. Her name became Elizabeth.

Leslie, however, never really cared for Ann's mother, and the feeling was mutual. So they just tolerated each other.

A long winter in Winnipeg became even longer.

10

Trip of a Lifetime

*A*nn had recently been thinking about Zoli's numerous invitations to visit him and his family in Long Beach, California. She thought this would be a great way to get her family to spend some time together, and for her husband to realize how wonderful his family really was. She worked up the courage to talk to Leslie about her desire to go on this trip.

"Think about it," she said. "This would be such a fantastic adventure. We could take our camping equipment, which would save us money on hotels, and we could sightsee on the way down there. Plus, my mother would like to see her son. This would be a trip of a lifetime for her."

After considering her idea, Leslie agreed to go on the trip. Because he was extremely precise in everything he did, he planned out their itinerary for every day. Leslie didn't know they would have so much fun that there would be no time to follow his plan.

A few weeks later, they set off on their journey. They drove through the Rockies and spent their first night in Banff, Calgary. The views of the jagged, snow-capped peaks were breathtaking, and they had never seen mountains so beautiful!

A stop at Lake Louise was next. This alpine lake, known for its sparkling aqua water, was situated at the base of a huge glacier between snow-covered peaks that had long been at the heart of Canadian mountaineering. As they enjoyed views of other glaciers through the passes, they stopped several times a day to take pictures.

Ann was overtaken with joy to be able to give her children this wonderful experience, and seeing the beautiful sights on their way out of the country made them appreciate Canada even more. Vancouver, British Columbia, was the last stop before they headed further south into the United States through the state of Washington.

Washington and Oregon had breathtaking scenery as well, and they stopped occasionally to wonder in amazement at God's creation. The biggest surprise was when they entered Northern California. The historical stretch of Highway 101 twisted and turned through the world's oldest and largest redwood forest. They saw trees that were the tallest living things in the world, prompting them to stop, get out of the car, and stare in awe at the incredibly beautiful forest.

One tree stood out from the rest because of its intriguing shape. This towering tree had one root system with seven trees growing out of it in a semicircle. Right next to this unusual tree was a bench, and Ann sat down to rest. There was a stand next to the bench with a button on it. When she pushed it, she heard a woman's sweet, melodious voice singing a beautiful song. Some of the lyrics spoke to her heart, such as *God is there with you, protecting you.*

Ann believed this was a message from an angel. She called the children over to listen to the song, hoping the lyrics would have the same impact on them as they had on her.

They soon arrived in San Francisco and experienced a different kind of beauty. The famous city was full of white buildings, but there were also houses on the hills painted in pastel colors. San Francisco was an elegant, tasteful metropolis that made a lasting impression on Ann and her family.

Their enthusiasm was stifled, however, by the cool evening temperatures. They felt like they were freezing in the damp fog that hovered over San Francisco Bay. The Canadian winters didn't seem much worse than this.

The weather warmed up as they approached Los Angeles. Zoli met them just outside the sprawling city so they could follow him to his house in Long Beach. Since this was their first trip to California, Zoli knew that there was no way Ann and the family could find their way around with all the freeways. One wrong turn, and they would be many miles from where they wanted to go.

They arrived at Zoli's place exhausted but were ready to continue their adventure the next day. They were happy to finally meet Zoli's wife, Nancy, and their two-year-old son, Victor.

The first stop, of course, was Disneyland. They had heard so much about "The Happiest Place on Earth," that they could hardly wait to get inside the amusement park. They all headed toward Fantasyland, and they felt like they were living out a fantasy. Nick and Susan were finally experiencing what most of the kids in America had taken for granted all their lives. They were amazed by all the sights and sounds, laughing and stepping onto as many rides as they could, eating cotton candy, and acting as if they were all five years old.

After taking a few days to rest, they visited Knott's Berry Farm, which was quite different from Disneyland, but it was still an exciting experience for the whole family. Zoli also took them to downtown Los Angeles, Hollywood, and Chinatown. Their relative gave the family a tour of a lifetime in six days.

They departed L.A. and headed to Las Vegas on a route that would eventually take them back to Canada. They wanted to take a different route home so they could see as many sights as possible on the way back. The zillions of lights on the famous Las Vegas Strip took their breath away as well as the garish casinos. Not in their wildest dreams had they ever pictured anything like this. Ann, Leslie, Nick, Susan, and Elizabeth walked around in wonderment at this storyland for adults. The lights and action everywhere nearly overwhelmed them.

Of course, the adults had to try a little gambling. They loved hearing the *ching-ching* of the slot machines when they won a few quarters. Elizabeth was hooked immediately, and Ann had to drag her away from the "one-arm bandits."

A Natural Wonder

Next on their itinerary was one of the seven natural wonders of the world—the Grand Canyon. The Grand Canyon is widely known for its exceptional beauty and is considered to be one of the world's most visually powerful landscapes. This natural wonder is noted for its plunging depths and unbelievable colors, especially at sunset. Scenic wonders within the park include high plateaus, plains, deserts, forests, streams, waterfalls, lava flows, and way down at the bottom of the canyon—the Colorado River. The twists and turns of this famous river continue for more than 275 miles.

The family agreed that the Grand Canyon was the most awe-inspiring and naturally beautiful sight they had seen on their whole trip. Ann got more enjoyment out of watching the faces of her children light up than any of the other wondrous sights. During the trip, she forgot how miserable the last couple of years had been and received a welcome break from constantly wondering where her husband was.

After a good night's rest in their tent, it was time to continue their journey. They drove through Yellowstone National Park, a vast natural forest covering nearly 9,000 square kilometers. Most of the forest was in Wyoming, a small part was in Montana, and only 1 percent stretches into Idaho. Yellowstone contains half of all the world's known geothermal features with more than 10,000 examples and more than 300 geysers—about two-thirds of the total on earth. There were numerous breathtaking waterfalls and great herds of wildlife, some of which were near extinction.

As they were driving on one of the roads, Nick screamed out, "Look out, there is a huge bear on the road!"

Leslie pulled over to the side of the road. He told Ann, "Get your camera. This is great. We'll get a nice close up." Of course, they were too afraid to get out of the car, so they sat mesmerized as this huge animal explored the outside of their car before sauntering away.

Their last stop was the Theodore Roosevelt National Park in South Dakota. Carved into the granite face of Mount Rushmore, a sheer peak rising 6,000 feet in the Black Hills, were the colossal images of four U.S. Presidents: George Washington, Thomas Jefferson, Abraham Lincoln, and Theodore Roosevelt. In paying tribute to them, the national memorial also commemorated the growth of the United States through the early part of the 20th century. The carvings were an incredible engineering feat, and the monument was constructed over the course of fourteen years. Unique among world sculptures and practically immune to the ravages of time and nature, Mount Rushmore stood as an enduring tribute to the genius sculptor Gutzon Borglum.

Saying goodbye to the U.S. Presidents and also to America, the family drove back across the border to Canada with their heads still spinning. They had a lot to digest.

All the interesting and educational things they had seen over three weeks had definitely made this a trip of a lifetime!

11

Another Big Trip

*S*usan had been seeing a young man who was three years older than she was, and she could hardly wait to get back from the California trip to see him. She thought she was deeply in love, but in reality, she was desperately seeking attention from a male figure since she never got any affection from her father, who never told her he loved her. Susan needed to be loved, and she was in love with the idea of love. She discovered that she could get it from this young man.

He was quite handsome, and he gave her all the attention that she wanted and more. She was head-over-heels in love with him, not knowing that eventually he would break her heart and leave her. Ann and Leslie did not approve of this relationship, however, because they were afraid it would only lead to trouble. When they got back from the trip, her parent's fears became reality.

Susan called her boyfriend as soon as they returned. "I have missed you so much," she exclaimed. "I can hardly wait to see you again!"

There was a long silence on the phone, then a sigh. "I don't think that would be a good idea. You see, I've been seeing someone else since you left."

Susan couldn't believe her ears. "It didn't take you long to forget about me, did it? How could you do that?"

He merely laughed it off. Apparently he didn't share the same feelings for Susan that she did for him. She was devastated and cried day and night. *How could he do this to me? I love him!* The first heartbreak is usually the hardest, and she thought she would never get over her first love.

She had so much trouble recovering from the break-up that her parents suggested she move in with her Uncle Zoli in California to get away from this young man for a while. They put Susan on a bus heading west, and she made the long four-day trip by herself at the age of seventeen. Because she left during winter, the bus had to travel through the snowbound Rockies.

Susan held her breath as the bus wound around sharp turns that overlooked long drops to the valley below. She had never been away from her parents, and she was extremely fearful of strangers. By the time she arrived in California, she was exhausted physically *and* mentally. Fortunately, she and her family had just been there a few months before, so she knew what to expect. Zoli and his wife picked her up and took her to their house, where they had a nice dinner waiting for her.

Nancy had just given birth to their second child, a little girl named Erika. Susan was happy to help with child care, cooking, and light housecleaning. She stayed with Zoli and his family for almost a year. Zoli then got her a job at a car dealership working as a secretary.

Zoli was learning to fly and had just received his pilot's license. He had been thinking about flying Susan to Canada for a visit. The thought of flying in a small airplane frightened Susan, however. She begged Zoli not to force her to fly in the little four-seat Cessna. But he insisted that she come along. "We'll go and surprise your parents. Don't you think they'd love that?" he asked.

"I'm sure they would, but I still don't want to make that long journey in such a small plane. I'm afraid I'll have motion sickness the whole time!" cried Susan.

"I'm responsible for you now, and I'm telling you that you *are* going!" Zoli shouted.

They asked Nancy's mother to come stay with the children. On a January day, Zoli, Nancy, and Susan took off from the Long Beach airport. As they got closer to Canada, everything was covered in snow since it was winter. While flying over North Dakota, Zoli noticed that he was running low on gas, so he made radio contact with an air traffic controller at a nearby airport. He got approval to land.

"I can't see the runway," Zoli said. He was searching for a small airport with only a few airplanes on the ground.

The dispatcher in the tower informed him, "Sir, you are above the airport. Do you see the runway?"

"I don't see a runway. Only a few airplanes. What are you talking about? You need to help me. I'm almost out of gas! Get us down from here!" There was panic in his voice now, which did not comfort Susan.

It had snowed the night before, and the airport maintenance crew hadn't cleared the snow from the runway. Zoli, taking a big chance, reduced his altitude as the tower dispatcher talked him down to the ground. When they got a couple of hundred feet above the runway, Susan yelled, "I see it, I see it! Look over to the right. There it is!"

Zoli made a safe landing, and they were all relieved to be on the ground. The rest of the trip went smoothly, and they really surprised Leslie, Ann, and Nick when they showed up in Winnipeg unannounced. They visited for a couple of days, then started their long journey back to California. Susan was especially happy when they finally touched down at the Long Beach Airport.

Eventually, Susan and a girlfriend moved into an apartment together. Susan experienced what it was like being on her own for the first time in her life. She had to budget her money because there was no more if she ran out. She had to take the bus to work since she could not afford a car, but living on her own was a great opportunity to learn how to be independent.

Nick Moves On

Nick lived with Ann and Leslie one more year while he finished high school. For his graduation gift, Ann surprised him with a trip to Niagara Falls for graduating with good grades. Leslie had to stay at home since he had to tend to the business. He did not mind since this meant he would have three weeks to do anything he wanted without anyone to answer to.

Ann and Nick planned their trip and got all their camping equipment together since they still could not afford to stay in a hotel. They would be gone for three weeks, and the expense of a hotel every night would have been beyond their means. When they said goodbye to Leslie, he made them promise they would be home in exactly three weeks. "I want you to walk into the house at 8 p.m. sharp that night," he chuckled.

The first part of the trip was long and boring until they crossed the border to the U.S. and were on the outskirts of Chicago. They both realized they were starving, so Nick took the first off-ramp he saw and drove to the nearest restaurant.

After they had been seated for a couple of minutes, a police officer walked in. He told the manager he was looking for the owner of a car with license plates from Winnipeg, Manitoba. Nick got scared, thinking he might be in trouble for speeding.

He gulped and raised his hand. "That would be our vehicle, officer."

The officer approached him and his mom. "Get your things together, and come with me immediately."

They obeyed, and when they got outside, they were surprised to receive some friendly advice from the officer. "Go up the street about ten blocks and look for another restaurant. This is a bad neighborhood, and it could be dangerous for you to hang around here."

Relieved and thankful, Ann and Nick got in the car and took off. They were a bit nervous after that incident, so they drove to Cleveland as fast as they could since they had some relatives who lived there. They spent a couple of days with them and got to see most of the points of local interest.

Ann and Nick were surprised to find that Cleveland was a mini-Hungary. They had no idea there was such a large Hungarian population in Cleveland. Everywhere they turned, they heard people speaking Hungarian.

Their next destination was Hackensack, New Jersey. They stayed with Ann's first cousin, Endre "Andy" Szalay, and his wife, Frida. Ann remembered when they were little children in Hungary and Andy came often to visit them. They had so much fun together, playing games and telling jokes. She also remembered Andy's beautiful mother, her aunt. She had a heart of gold and had always been kind to Ann.

Andy and Frida welcomed them with open arms and had a wonderful meal waiting for them. They stayed up half the night talking about their past and filling in the gaps from all the years they had not seen each other. During the four days Ann and Nick stayed with the Szalays, they ventured into New York City and got a grand tour of Manhattan. They had picked a perfect time to go to New York because the 1964 World Fair was in full swing.

Hailing itself as a "universal and international" exposition, the fair's theme was "Peace through Understanding" and was dedicated to "Man's Achievement on a Shrinking Globe in an Expanding Universe." A twelve-story stainless steel model of the Earth, the Unisphere, symbolized the theme. In spite of the international theme, American corporations dominated the exposition as exhibitors.

The state of New York hosted the fair at its $6 million open-air pavilion. Designed by famed modernist architect Philip Nickson, the pavilion also boasted the fair's high spot observation towers. The main floor of the pavilion was a large-scale design of a Texaco highway map of New York State.

Disneyland recreated the "It's a Small World" ride, "Great Moments with Mr. Lincoln," as well as the original Disneyland People Mover, based on the Ford Magic Skyway.

The fair was definitely a highlight of their trip until then, but it was time to head to Niagara Falls, on the route toward home. By the time they arrived, the sun had already set. They pitched their tent at a nearby campground and went to sleep. Ann and Nick awoke to see the most awesome sight they had ever seen. They had heard the roaring of the water all night, but when they walked outside and saw the awesome volume of water dropping to its depth, they just stood there with their mouths hanging open.

More than six million cubic feet of water fell over the crest line every minute. The Niagara Falls were formed when glaciers receded at the end of the last Ice Age, and water from the newly formed Great Lakes carved a path through the Niagara Escarpment en route to the Atlantic Ocean.

While not exceptionally high, the Niagara Falls are very wide. They are renowned not only for their beauty, but also as a valuable source of hydroelectric power. Managing the balance between recreational, commercial, and industrial uses had been a challenge for the stewards of the Niagara Falls since the 19th century.

Ann and Nick signed up for a tour, which was fascinating as well as frightful. They boarded an elevator that took them down to the depths of the falls. Before they were allowed to leave the elevator, they were all given raincoats and boots. The tour guide led them on a path that was behind part of the falls, where they saw this majestic beauty from the backside. What power! They could just feel the energy soaring out of this mass of water.

Ann and Nick spent one more night at Niagara Falls, then departed for home. They had no idea how long it would take to drive to Winnipeg, which was 1,500 miles away.

They drove all day and arrived in Toronto in the evening. After spending the night there, they set off for Winnipeg the next morning. They had promised Leslie that they would be home precisely at 8 p.m. on this day. They pulled into Winnipeg about 6 p.m., so they killed a couple of hours just to be true to their promise.

Precisely at 8 o'clock, Ann and Nick walked through the front door. Leslie was shocked because he never actually expected them to arrive *exactly* on time after such a long cross-country trip.

12

The Empty Nest Years

*A*nn's mother, Elizabeth, soon decided that she didn't care for the weather in Winnipeg. She continuously talked about Zoli and how fortunate he was to live in California, where the Mediterranean climate was mild most of the year.

Nick planned to go to college and major in electronic engineering. Imagine that—the best school he could find for his course of study was at Long Beach State in Southern California. He was getting sick and tired of the cold weather in Canada, and his feelings intensified when Susan sent him pictures of being out by the pool in January. He approached his mom and dad and told them about his desire to go to school in Southern California, which pulled at Ann's heartstrings.

"If you go to college in America, we will not see you for four years," she said.

"Maybe longer," he replied. "I'm never coming back to Canada. I'm sick and tired of shoveling snow!"

So within a few months, Nick *and* his grandmother moved to Long Beach. Susan had been happy to hear that another part of the family would be living in California. She immediately found an apartment that the three of them could live in together. When Nick and Elizabeth arrived, she had the apartment all set up. She loved the new arrangement, and since she was sharing the cost with two other people, her financial situation improved.

Ann and Leslie were not as content, however. They found themselves alone for the first time in many years. This was the start of the empty nest years, and Ann wasn't happy about it at all.

I can't be stuck here in this cold weather with a man I don't have anything in common with anymore. I've got to be with my children! Who is this person I'm married to anyway?

They worked together at the printing shop and kept up the appearance of being a married couple. Ann's heart had not been in their marriage for a long time. She didn't feel "needed" at home, now that her children didn't live there anymore, and she soon became lonely and miserable.

Ann started reminiscing about the early years of her marriage. Back then, she rushed home from teaching and started putting together whatever food they had for dinner. She was just learning how to cook, and it took a lot of concentration for her to get all the ingredients organized and follow the recipe.

Every time she was in the midst of preparing something, Leslie would come into the kitchen and interrupt her. "Listen to this poem," he'd say. "This is so fascinating. You will love it!"

Ann could have cared less. She didn't like poetry, especially when she was trying to cook something. When they were newlyweds, she had taken the time to stop what she was doing and listen to him intently as if she was really interested. But that was a long time ago.

Leslie had never taken an interest in doing any of the things Ann enjoyed, like going on walks, swimming in a pool, or any sort of physical activity. Whenever they had been obligated to attend a social event that included dancing, he never asked her to dance even though he knew full well how she loved it. He sat in the corner with the men and talked about politics.

When Ann was young, her parents taught her to play bridge. Every evening the family would get together and play bridge or some other card game for hours. She missed playing card games very much, but Leslie never wanted to play *any* card games. He thought they were a waste of time. In the evenings, he read every chance he got, sometimes until well past midnight. Ann was unable to get her rest for the next day's work because the light in the bedroom kept her awake.

As her mind returned to her present situation, she realized that this man she had been living with for more than twenty years had absolutely nothing in common with her, except for their children. Now that Susan and Nick were gone, she wasn't sure that she could stay in Canada alone with this man much longer. She longed to be where the rest of her family was.

She made up her mind about what they should do. One day, she approached Leslie and pleaded, "I strongly believe we should sell the business and the house and move to California, where the rest of our family is. I hope you agree with me because I'm miserable here in Winnipeg. The weather is terrible, and I miss my family."

Leslie, to her surprise, was open to the idea. "We have our dream house, and our business that we built from nothing is doing well. While it would be hard to give all that up, I do see your reasoning."

Ann wasn't sure that Leslie would leave the women he had relationships with in Winnipeg, however. But she knew that he loved his family very much—in his own way—so she hoped he would agree to move.

Leslie did eventually consent, and they started the paperwork to get their visas and green cards so they could move to America. Ann kept thinking about what Nick had said about never coming back to Canada. She remembered how Nick's comments as a child influenced their decision to leave Hungary. Now, his decision to leave Canada was one of the main reasons she wanted to also leave.

Their friends, most of whom were Hungarians, were extremely disappointed to hear about their decision to move to California. There were ten couples they had gotten very close to in the past eight years.

One of Ann's friends informed her, "We're going to throw you and Leslie a going-away party. It will be at our house on Saturday." The party was great. Ann and Leslie received some beautiful presents that they could remember their friends by. When it was time to leave, Leslie was still lingering because he could not finish talking about politics.

That's when one of Ann's friends whispered in her ear, "There goes the town cock!" as she pointed at Leslie.

Ann knew exactly what her friend meant by that. She was just shocked that it was such a well-known fact among their friends.

Obviously, her husband hadn't been very good at hiding his affairs.

13

Helping Hands

*A*nn and Leslie finally received their visas to move to the United States. They now had their green cards, which made them permanent residents and would allow them to work legally.

Ann was the first to move to Long Beach. Leslie had to stay behind to sell the house and the business. Ann, Elizabeth, Susan, and Nick all got an apartment together.

Nick drove an old, run-down car that needed repairs all the time. Zoli introduced Nick to one of his buddies who owned an auto dealership. He immediately asked Nick how much money he had to buy a new car. "I only have $250. I'm sorry, but I do not have any more," Nick answered.

The owner of the dealership pointed to a used Dodge Royal. "Would you like this car? An old couple just traded it in for a new car. It has four new tires and runs well. If you want it, it's yours for $250."

"Would I like this car? Are you kidding me? I would love it, but I can't believe you will let me have it for only $250!"

Nick paid for the car and drove around all day. He couldn't believe that he finally had such a cool car. As he was driving around, he started thinking how the Anglican Church members had helped his family in Canada. Now, a total stranger had helped him, a college student on a budget, buy a reliable car for less than it was worth. It was nice to know there were good people in the world.

Susan had a similar situation happen to her at the car dealership where she worked. She had been taking the bus to work every day, and one morning the sales manager saw her get off the bus. He asked her, "How much money do you have on you, Susan?"

She looked in her purse and found that she had $25. Not knowing what he wanted, she asked, "Did you want to borrow some? I only have $25."

The manager replied, "No, I just want you to give it to me so I can officially sell you this old Renault. It was just traded in, and it's yours if you're interested."

Susan gasped with surprise. "You can't be serious. I can't believe that you'll sell me a car for $25!"

They filled out the paperwork, and the manager handed her the pink slip, along with the keys to the car. Now her transportation problems were solved. Susan was relieved that she didn't have to take the bus anymore. This was unbelievable, and she felt blessed to have been treated so kindly.

Ann immediately looked for a job, and found one in offset printing. The company made humorous greeting cards, and Ann thought this would be a fun job. When she was being interviewed, the owners asked her how old she was and what kind of car she drove.

"I don't understand why it is important for you to know what kind of car I drive and how old I am. But if you really must know, I'm thirty-nine, and I drive a 1964 Chevy. What difference does that make?"

One of the owners replied, "If you were younger than thirty-nine, you might have child-care problems. Are you sure you're thirty-nine? All women are thirty-nine. I also noticed an accent, and if you drove a VW, I would know you're German, and we don't hire Germans."

That's when Ann realized that her bosses were Jewish and had some strict rules they lived and worked by.

Ann started work the next day, and now she was set in her new life. Leslie sold the business and the house within a few months, and he joined the family by December of that same year. He found a job at a printing company, and fortunately for him, it was the kind of position where he could go in anytime and leave anytime, as long as he got the work done.

One night, Ann thought about what had happened the past couple of months. *Nick got help buying a car so he would have transportation. Susan doesn't have to take the bus anymore because she got a car that runs for $25. Leslie and I were both able to find jobs immediately.*

Ann was amazed. One day she asked Susan, "Do you realize that God is watching over us and pointing us in the right direction? He loves us and carries us in His arms during difficult times. He is always there."

Just when Ann thought everything was going well, something happened to shake her faith. After Zoli had his pilot's license for several years, he decided to become an instructor. He loved flying, and it was the only thing he was passionate about— besides swimming. He had many students, and through the years he earned the reputation of being an outstanding teacher. He was well known at the airports and often got word-of-mouth referrals.

On a beautiful summer day, he and one of his students were practicing "touch and go" maneuvers, which is one of the many necessary skills his student would have to perform in order to become a licensed pilot. The pilot is required to take off, make a loop, just barely touch down for a landing, and then take off again.

As they left the hanger that morning, the tower cleared them to move onto a particular runway. When they taxied onto the runway, a huge passenger jet pulled in front of them on the same runway since the airline pilot had received clearance from the tower as well.

The power of the jets created such a tremendous force, Zoli's plane immediately flipped upside down and burst into flames. Zoli remained calm and remembered the emergency training he took to become an instructor. He calmly gave instructions to his student. "We are both going to open our doors at the same time. I want you to hold your breath and run as fast as you can through the flames!"

"No, I can't do that," yelled the student. "There's no way I'm running through those flames! Are you crazy?"

"Do you want to die? That's what's going to happen if you stay in this plane. It's going to blow up any second! I'm going. You better do the same!"

Zoli opened his door, and the student followed his example. The draft of the flames bolted through the cabin. Zoli covered his head with his jacket, held his breath, and ran through the scorching flames. He was scared to death, thinking that this could be his last few seconds on earth.

His dash seemed like an eternity, but within seconds he was finally out in the open, and he could draw a deep breath again. The pants he had been wearing were polyester, and they melted on his legs, but his wool sweater saved his upper body from getting too badly burned. As he regained his senses, he realized that he had survived this accident with relatively minor injuries. Although he did have pain in his legs, he was grateful that he had been able to run out of the plane.

He looked around to see where his student was. He could not see him anywhere, so he started running around the huge flames, screaming and calling his name. "Oh, my God! He is in there somewhere burning up! Help, help, somebody help us!"

As he searched the ground, he saw the student lying in the fire, most of his body in flames. Zoli responded without thinking and grabbed the student with his bare hands. He pulled him out of the flames and dragged him to safety. Zoli then removed his sweater and used it to smother the flames on the student's body, screaming for help at the same time.

By the time the fire trucks arrived, Zoli had put out the flames that engulfed the student. The firemen quickly placed the badly burned young man on a gurney, then they all ran away from the plane. Within seconds, the aircraft exploded into bits, and the sky was filled with smoke and debris.

A few hours later, Ann got a phone call and was told that her brother had been in a serious accident. The whole family rushed over to the burn center in Sherman Oaks to find Zoli bandaged up. His head was swollen to almost twice its size. His lips were charcoal black, but his lungs were not damaged because he was able to hold his breath for so long. The skills he learned as a swimmer had served him well. His hands were completely shriveled, however, because of the first-degree burns he received while trying to put out the fire on his student's body.

The student was not as fortunate as Zoli. Most of his body was badly burned beyond recognition. He had to go through several skin grafts and major plastic surgery to regain some human characteristics. Thanks to Zoli's quick wits and courage, though, he survived. He would be eternally grateful to Zoli for saving his life.

Zoli and the student pilot filed a joint lawsuit, which lasted several years. They eventually received monetary compensation, and after paying their attorney, the pair ended up with a generous and well-deserved sum of money.

Zoli recovered from his burns, but his hair grew back white. Several months later, after the layers had peeled off, the skin on his face was as smooth as a baby's skin. Basically it was a facial peel, just achieved in an agonizing manner. Zoli underwent several skin grafts on his hands, but he regained full use of most of his fingers.

All in all, Zoli knew he was very lucky to be alive. He was back flying airplanes within several months after his accident because nothing was going to keep him on the ground. He eventually bought a small, rundown airport in the California desert town of Hesperia that included a small motel, which he and his wife ran for many years.

Many of Zoli's flight students were well-to-do, and one afternoon three of them approached him with a proposition. "Zoli, how would you like to fly us to Europe?" asked a fellow named George.

"Are you kidding me?" Zoli replied. "Do you know what kind of an airplane we would need to fly to Europe over the Atlantic?"

"No problem!" George reassured him. "Just tell us the kind of airplane that will get us there, and it's done. You only have to worry about flying the aircraft."

It had been ten years since the accident when Zoli and his three students took off from the Long Beach Airport in a seven-passenger Twin Beach Tail-dragger. They were headed for Europe. Hopefully there would be no complications.

The plane could hold enough fuel to fly for 1,200 miles, so they knew they would have to stop about every 900 to 1,000 miles. Zoli was the pilot and all three students took turns being the co-pilot.

This adventure didn't cost Zoli a penny since his students paid for the fuel and other expenses. They hopscotched from Halifax to Iceland to Scotland. When they landed safely in Budapest a few days later, Zoli kissed the ground, thankful for the safe arrival. Their European trip was something that Zoli and his students would never forget.

After returning from Europe, Zoli got into the automobile business. He bought old cars, fixed them up, and sold them. By this time, he had been married five times, and his latest wife, Beatrix, was getting tired of all his "career" changes.

Zoli's marriage to Beatrix lasted seventeen years—the longest one yet—but she left him.

Zoli was on his own again.

14

Taking the Pledge

*A*fter Leslie moved to Long Beach, Elizabeth decided to move out and live on her own. She had been working at a Beverly Hills mansion as a supervisor for the gardener and the housekeeper. She had learned the routes to take the bus wherever she needed to go, so she had become quite independent.

Elizabeth cleaned her own apartment, cooked for herself, and eventually furnished her new place quite nicely. She met some Hungarian ladies in the neighborhood, so she even started making friends. Once a week, she and her friends got together and play bridge, speaking the language of their home country.

After being in the U.S. for five years, Elizabeth attended night school to prepare for the American citizenship test. She could barely speak English, however, and being older made it much more difficult to learn and retain the necessary information. Her instructor gave her fifty-two sample questions, and she memorized every one of them. She didn't understand half of what she learned, but she had the questions and answers memorized.

Ann, her mother Elizabeth, and Zoli in 1967

Elizabeth wanted to become a U.S. citizen because she was so grateful to be able to live in this wonderful country. There were about twenty-five people in her class, and everyone was nervous about taking the test. As soon as the instructor said the number of the question and read it, she mumbled to herself, mentally going down the list of practice questions in order. When she got to the one they were on, her face lit up in recognition, and Elizabeth proudly yelled out the answer word for word.

The instructor only asked three questions, and each time she put her hand up and answered the question correctly. The instructor was stunned because he had never seen anyone so determined to give the precise answers. She was immediately awarded her citizenship and congratulated for her hard work. Zoli was there with her, and proudly told the family how well she aced the test.

Elizabeth had always set a good example for everyone who knew her. She was full of love and always there to lend a helping hand. Since she was from a well-to-do family in Hungary, she had been taught as a child how to behave in public, including having perfect manners.

Elizabeth was always busy with something. If she didn't have work to do, she crocheted or sewed curtains, Asian rugs, and new clothes. Her sewing machine was always set up for whatever project she was working on.

When she was young, she had a beautiful voice and loved to sing. She also loved to play the piano. Some evenings, her husband would lock the piano room door and play the violin while Elizabeth sang beautifully for several hours. Ann and her siblings were not allowed to even get close to that room when their parents were in there.

Elizabeth had an easy life when she was younger, but as an older person, she held her own and knew how to work for a living. All her life she had attended a Catholic church, and by example she showed people that God gave her the strength and will to go on. She knew that He was with her all the time.

This was never more evident than when she prepared for the U.S. citizenship test. If there was ever a time she needed a miracle, it was then, and she received it.

15

Something Goes Wrong

*L*eslie was enjoying his job since he could come and go as he pleased. He had never handled discipline well and didn't like being told when to go to work. He always said showing up for work was like being in the army — you're given orders and told what to do all day.

In 1967, he started working for a Hungarian newspaper in Los Angeles part time. He wrote several articles each week and was finally doing what he really loved. Leslie could freely speak out against Communism and get out all his pent-up feelings. He became editor of the newspaper, and in no time, readers loved his columns. His name got to be well known in the Hungarian community.

He spent more time writing, which earned little, than working at the printing company. Once again, Leslie was stubbornly doing what he wanted. His meager salary and Ann's pay were barely enough for them to get by, but Leslie never had much drive to make money. He just wanted to do what pleased him. Later in life, though, he won several awards for his writing and was honored at a banquet for all his hard work at the newspaper.

Ann's job, on the other hand, was more disciplined. She had to be at work at 8 a.m. sharp and work eight hours. Her commute was twenty-six miles each way, which made her days very long. She was fortunate that the owners treated her with respect and appreciated her hard work. She couldn't recall enjoying a job more, so she ended up working there for eleven years. Even though bending over a light table for hours at a time and developing the negatives in a dark room was hard work, it was rewarding.

One day she had to work overtime to get everything ready for the printer the next morning. She called Leslie at home and told him she would be late. Exhausted after ten hours of leaning over a table, her eyes strained, she arrived at home about 8 o'clock. Dinner was not waiting for her, of course, but a cruel attack was.

"You could have come up with a better excuse than having to work overtime! You have never had to stay late!" Leslie yelled at her accusingly. "I suppose you were working hard with your supervisor! Or maybe, you weren't even *at* work!"

Ann just stood there speechless, not believing her ears. Even though she was exhausted and hungry, she couldn't ignore being falsely accused. "If you don't believe me, that is your problem. I'm telling the truth!" she retorted.

Ann went to bed without eating anything and then woke up at dawn to drive the twenty-six miles to work to be there in time to supervise the printers. Most of the printers were Mexican and didn't speak much English, but Ann, having been in the same situation, knew how to communicate with all of them. Before long, she knew all about their families, and they knew about hers.

When Ann got home the following night, her husband did not say a word to her. In fact, he did not speak to her for over a week, as if he was the injured one.

The silent treatment was new to her. So were the times when Leslie went with her everywhere, except work, and would not let her out of his sight. On one occasion, she needed a pair of shoes, so he accompanied her to the mall and waited outside the store while she tried on and purchased a new pair of shoes.

"Does it take this long to pay for a pair of shoes?" he demanded when she stepped out of the store. "I was watching you. The salesman must have whispered something to you because I saw you smiling at him and saying something back to him. I'm sure you two made plans to meet somewhere!"

Once again, Ann was taken aback by this strange accusation. She didn't know how to handle it. "You have no idea what you're talking about," she shot back. "None of it is true! What kind of person do you think I am?"

That prompted another couple of weeks of the silent treatment from Leslie.

One afternoon, Elizabeth stopped by to visit. Ann told her mother what had been happening. Her mother knew there was something wrong with Leslie and had sensed it for a while. That night when Leslie came home, she smacked him on his head as hard as she could.

"How dare you treat my daughter like this? Who do you think you are?"

Leslie grabbed her hand to stop her from hitting him. "Nobody has ever hit me in my life! Don't you *ever* do that again!"

"That's your problem. Somebody should have smacked you forty years ago!"

Leslie came up with an idea to "save" their marriage. He brought home pornographic movies for them to watch together. Since he was convinced that Ann was cheating on him, he thought watching porn would bring them closer together.

After about the sixth film, Ann told him, "I don't want to see any more of these horrible movies. I can't stand to watch another one! What are you trying to accomplish?"

"I'm trying to get you in the mood. I need more than you. You will do this!" Leslie demanded.

"If watching porn brings you happiness, go ahead, but don't expect me to watch with you. We have three TVs, so I'll watch something else in the other room."

The next thing Leslie did was purchase erotic books with lots of pictures, which he would thumb through every night, one after the other.

After a few days he confronted Ann with a proposition. "These books are telling me that if we bring another person into our relationship, we could spice up our marriage."

Ann thought for a minute, and then came up with a brilliant response. "All right, we'll do it, but the third person has to be a man!" Leslie never brought up the subject again.

Ann believed marriage was a holy institution between a man and a woman who were deeply in love. She was taught that the consummation of marriage and the commitment to a life together was sacred. She deeply loved Leslie when they got married and wanted to spend the rest of her life with him. He was the only man she wanted to have a sexual relationship with, but apparently he did not feel the same way. He was only interested in his own gratification.

A few weeks passed by when Ann received a phone call from Leslie. He was calling from the Long Beach Police Station.

"Come get me right away. I've been arrested!" Leslie pleaded. "You need to bail me out. It'll cost $52 to get me out."

"Why! What have you done?"

"I'll tell you later. Just hurry. The police are lying!"

When Ann arrived at the police station, they informed her that Leslie was showing his private parts in a public park. She could not believe her ears, so she asked them to explain it again.

On the way home in the car, his story was different. "I had to urinate badly, so I went behind a tree, but a policeman was watching. He walked up to me and arrested me. Don't they have better things to do?" he asked innocently.

After they arrived home, they had a long conversation about the incident, and he finally admitted that he went to the park quite frequently because he liked to watch young couples making love in the bushes.

Life with Leslie was becoming unbearable. He didn't work as much as he should have, he was obsessed with his sexual fantasies, and he continuously questioned Ann's whereabouts.

16

The Tide Turns

*A*nn approached Leslie one day, hoping to salvage what was left of their marriage. "Would you be willing to go to a marriage counselor?" she asked.

She did not trust her husband anymore, nor was she convinced that he wasn't cheating on her as he claimed. Ann thought he was searching for something, but she had no idea how to help him. She was confident a professional therapist could make some sense of their relationship.

The marriage counselor saw them separately for two visits, and then on the third visit they went together. Leslie shared something with the counselor that took Ann by surprise.

"I love my wife," he began. "I cannot stand the idea that she could belong to someone else. I love to see her beautiful face as I satisfy her needs. I know she loves me, but I feel something is missing. For instance when we're watching a movie, I notice that she's looking at the actor's crotch. I think maybe she's fantasizing about him."

Ann sat there, stunned by what he had to say. She had no response. This was beyond normal. There was something seriously wrong here. What Leslie said was absolutely not true!

This type of behavior went on for two more years—the attacks, the insults, and the jealousy. Ann was totally worn out emotionally. It was a good thing that Nick and Susan had gotten apartments of their own because she had no energy to deal with anything else.

One summer, one of Ann's nephews came to visit from Hungary. He was touring the world and asked if he could stay with Ann and Leslie for a week while he checked out the sights in Los Angeles. Alex had just turned twenty-one, and he was excited to explore this famous city.

"Of course," Ann said. Over family dinners, they talked about his adventures and things he had seen in Los Angeles that day.

When the nephew left, Leslie verbally attacked Ann. "You cannot deny this one—I saw you two together!" he exclaimed.

"You mean, Alex?" Ann couldn't believe her ears. "Wh-what did you see? Wh-what are you talking about?" Ann was stuttering because this was just too much.

"One morning, when Alex was sitting in the arm-chair, you were on your knees in front of him when I looked into the room."

"You're absolutely crazy! I was cleaning the floor and probably bent down to pick something up. I don't even know how to respond to this! He's twenty-one years old, for gosh sakes. My son is twenty-three. Are you accusing me of being with someone who could be my child? Do you think I'm that sick?"

Leslie wouldn't let up. "You're lying, but if you admit it, I will forgive you. You are mine, and you will never belong to anyone else. Would you be willing to take a lie detector test to prove that you haven't been cheating?"

Shocked, Ann could only say, "So, we have sunk this low. We have come to the deepest level of the other side of trust. Yes, I will take a lie detector test, if it will get you get off my back and make you stop torturing me! You have been treating me extremely unfair, and your attitude has been cold and cruel!"

Ann had never felt so ashamed in her life when the lie detector technician started placing all the wires on her head and her chest. A total stranger was asking her extremely personal and intimate questions. He told her to answer with short answers and no long stories.

Rage and shame started to overcome her. *Why should I have to suffer such humiliation?* She was ready to smack the technician over the head with his machine and run out of there, but she took control of herself and realized she had nothing to hide. She endured the test until the end.

When they were done, the technician turned to Leslie and said, "This woman has never cheated on you in her life."

As Ann and Leslie got into the car to go home, she had only one thing to say to Leslie. "As soon as we get home, get your things together. Take whatever you want and leave because you are not staying another night in my home! I have nothing else to say to you, and I want nothing more to do with you either!"

There was only silence all the way home. Leslie was shocked at her demands. He packed up some clothes and other belongings, but before he left, he started crying. "I only did what I did because I love you so much," he said. "You know how bad my eyes are getting. I could go blind, so what's to become of me without you?"

Ann was not deterred at his play for sympathy. "You should have thought of that before. Get out of my life—now!"

17

Calling on Her Faith

*A*nn was left alone for the first time in her life, emotionally battered and broken. She had a job and probably could support herself, but questions kept running though her head.

What will happen to me?
Did I make the right decision?
Who can I talk to?

It was strange to her that she didn't have to take care of Leslie. She no longer had to cook him dinner or wash his clothes. Now she only had to worry about herself and what *she* wanted. She did not tell Nick or Susan about what had happened, however. They lived far enough away, and they had their own lives. Ann did not want to burden them with her problems.

As the weeks turned into months, she started to enjoy her freedom. She didn't have anyone to report to, she didn't have to have dinner ready at a certain time, and she could do anything she pleased without getting criticized. She continued to work and put all that she had into her job. Her supervisors appreciated her effort.

She would think about Leslie from time to time, wondering how he was getting along. Their twenty-fifth wedding anniversary was a few months away. The thought that she and Leslie would not celebrate it together saddened her because she had different plans for this special occasion. She finally told her children and her friends that she had asked Leslie to move out, and they were understanding and supportive. Ann did not give anyone details, however, because she was ashamed of how her husband had been behaving. She started going to church more often, where she got the strength she needed from God to move on. She started sleeping better since there was no one to fear anymore.

What Ann didn't know at that time was that her husband was suffering from serious mental conditions. For instance, Leslie was suffering from insane jealousy, which is the fixed belief that one's partner is unfaithful and sexually cheating on him behind his back.

Ann began reading about the subject and found some helpful information:

The belief of an insanely jealous person regarding the unfaithfulness of his partner is not founded in reality. Insanely jealous people will go out of their way to prove that their partner is cheating, which includes interrogation of the partner, repeated telephone calls to work and surprise visits, stalking behavior, or hiring a private detective to follow the partner. Jealous individuals may search the partner's clothes and possessions, scrutinize diaries and correspondence, and examine bed linens, underclothes, and even genitalia for evidence of sexual activity.

The accused partner is assumed to be guilty until evidence of innocence is found, but this cannot materialize. This belief of infidelity is firmly entrenched and unshakable. Any counter evidence, assertion of faithfulness, or pledge of undivided love on the part of the accused partner does not appease his anger or suspicion. The question of the faithfulness of the spouse becomes an obsession for a person gripped with insane jealousy.

An insanely jealous person imagines acts of unfaithfulness committed by one's spouse. He may suspect a familiar person as a potential rival or he may imagine an unknown rival. He is convinced that he is right to be jealous even when the evidence does not support his beliefs. It is very difficult to show him the truth.

Since Leslie was convinced that he was right, he was probably also suffering from paranoid schizophrenia, Ann learned. One primary way of determining the difference between irrational jealousy and paranoia is that the person with delusions firmly believes the reality of that belief, whereas an individual with irrational jealousy is more likely to say, "I know I'm being unreasonable and that it's creating problems, but I just can't help it. That's how I feel."

Since Leslie was always more concerned about his own comfort and his own needs, it could be said that he was also narcissistic. Ann continued to read:

Narcissistic personality disorder is a mental disorder in which people have an inflated sense of their own importance and a deep need for admiration. Those with narcissistic personality disorder believe that they're superior to others and have little regard for other people's feelings or needs. But behind this mask of ultra-confidence lies a fragile self-esteem, vulnerable to the slightest criticism.

Leslie was living in a one-bedroom apartment and totally miserable. He could not handle being alone with no one to take care of him. He kept imagining all the things Ann was probably doing, now that she was all alone. He hired a private detective to follow her wherever she went. Of course, the detective had nothing to report, so finally Leslie put a stop to that, probably thinking that the detective had made a move on Ann.

He decided to go back to Hungary and visit relatives since he was so lonely. He had a layover in New York, so he planned to look up Ann's cousin, Andy Szalay, who lived in New Jersey. He stayed with them overnight, and they had long talks about what was happening with Leslie and Ann. Leslie tearfully informed them that his wife had been cheating on him, and he had to get away. Andy and his wife tried to comfort him as much as possible, but they both had a hard time believing that Ann would do anything that Leslie was accusing her of.

Andy had known Ann all his life and knew she had strong morals. He also knew how important her wedding vows had been to her, so he took Leslie's story with a grain of salt. He did not call Ann to tell her because he thought the whole idea was so bizarre. It wasn't until forty-two years later, two years after Leslie's death, that Andy would share with Ann what Leslie had told them so many years ago.

While back in Hungary, Leslie described to his relatives how he had been abused and how betrayed by Ann. Of course, this didn't get back to Ann for many years because all the relatives knew what kind of person Ann was. They simply did not believe Leslie.

After Leslie returned to the U.S., he began to get more and more despondent. This went on for several months. He contacted Ann's brother, Zoli, and asked him to speak to Ann and try to talk her into at least meeting with him. Ann felt strong enough by then, so she agreed.

When Leslie showed up, they shook hands as if they were business partners, but within minutes Leslie was on his knees, sobbing. "I beg you to take me back. I miss you so much!" he cried. "I will never bring up the subject again, if you will just let me back in your life. I cannot live without you! I need you, our children, and our family life!"

Ann could not believe that the man who did nothing but hurt and criticize her was on his knees begging for forgiveness. She still had some feelings for him, even after all the verbal abuse and accusations she had received from him. She had been with him almost twenty-five years, and he was the father of her children. Divorce was still not an option for her.

She finally agreed that he could come back, but she did make one stipulation, "If you ever accuse me, or I feel any kind of jealousy from you, I will leave and that will be the last time! You tortured me for years. I was not the one who was unfaithful, so don't forget about Canada and your affairs. I'm not the one who got arrested for being an exhibitionist, so there better not be any accusations against me, ever again! If you understand this, and promise, then we can give it another chance! Do you understand?"

He nodded yes.

She added one more thing. "From now on, you will give me all your paychecks, and I will manage our money since you have no idea how to budget. I took care of the money in Canada, and we were able to build a house, and here we have nothing. If I take over the finances, maybe we can have a house here as well."

A few weeks after they reconciled, they celebrated their twenty-fifth wedding anniversary on July 20, 1969. This day has gone down in history, but not because of Ann and Leslie. This was the day that man landed on the moon for the first time.

They stayed together for forty more years. Leslie did not accuse Ann of infidelity, nor did he question her whereabouts until the last year of his life. They lived together as husband and wife and had family over for holidays, which they both loved. Their family was the one thing that held them together.

At Christmas, they could hardly wait for everyone to come to their house. It was a Hungarian tradition to celebrate Christmas Eve, more so than Christmas

Day, so Ann and Leslie always invited their kids and grandchildren to their house on Christmas Eve. Ann would work half a day on Christmas Eve, but she made sure she had all the favorite foods ready for her family by the time they came over.

She loved organizing the entertainment for the evening, and before Christmas, she spent many hours with her grandchildren practicing different skits and singing Christmas carols they could perform after dinner. Leslie would sometimes do magic shows because he loved to do tricks and impress his grandchildren.

Ann and Leslie loved their family and lived for the family gatherings, but the relationship between them was never the same again. Ann had lost most of the feelings she had for her husband, and she never wholly trusted him after they were reunited. Leslie suffered with his demons, but the fear of losing Ann gave him the strength not to bring up forbidden subjects.

Ann believed he really did love her—and really needed her—but he had a hard time showing any affection toward her. Ann would see old couples walking on the street, holding hands, or a man with his arm around his wife and wish she could get this kind of affection from her husband. Perhaps if she had known more about his mental illness, she could have coped with his oddities better.

One day, Zoli told her that he had lent $500 to Leslie months before because Leslie had been arrested again for exposing himself at Griffith Park.

Nothing surprised Ann anymore. She was calloused to his erratic sexual behaviors.

With Ann handling the finances, they finally did purchase a house. In 2003, after living in their home for thirty-two years, they sold it and moved into a brand new house in a gated community. They both loved their new home. Ann, who was now finally retired, immediately joined the bridge club and spent several hours in her garden every day. She went swimming any time she wanted and became good friends with women in the neighborhood.

Ann and Leslie before Honorary Dinner,
five months before Leslie's death

Honoring Leslie for his achievements
with the Hungarian newspaper

Leslie would stay at home and research topics like flying saucers. He also liked to find evidence to disprove anything in the Bible. Ann never did know how he really felt about God because he didn't like to talk about religion. He said that the subject was private for him.

After they had been together for almost forty more years, Leslie started to manifest some symptoms of his mental illness again. He could not control his irrational jealousy any longer. He started with his vicious attacks, questioning Ann whenever she was a few minutes late. He accused her of having a boyfriend who came into their house in the middle of the night.

Ann was eighty-four and Leslie was eighty-nine when this new round of accusations began. Ann did not know how to handle these attacks. She would just look at him in disbelief and shake her head. He was still watching porn movies and reading erotic books, but now he didn't even try to hide them from his wife. She was not aware that this behavior was a symptom of yet another mental illness her husband had. She wouldn't completely understand everything until after his death.

Three months after they celebrated their sixty-fifth wedding anniversary, Leslie passed away at the age of eighty-nine, a couple of months shy of his ninetieth birthday.

Nick thought his father was a kind man, and as he said in his dad's eulogy: *Leslie was an intellectual, a philosopher, and a loner. Above all, he was a dreamer. He imagined a world where he could make a difference through the power of the pen. Literature was his passion and his love in life. He lived in the twilight of reason, superstition, and pseudoscience, but he was sincere about his convictions to the end.*

Ann hoped he would rest in peace.

18

A Life-Changing Decision

*S*usan had dated several men during the time she was in Long Beach. Zoli had set her up with some of his friends' sons, but she had only gone on one date with most of them. She was looking for something, but wasn't quite sure what it was.

She was always drawn to a wild kind of man: outgoing, good looking, popular—a man who would take charge. She really didn't care what type of person he was as long as he gave her attention since she had gotten so little from her father. Susan was quite ignorant about men in general.

One beautiful summer day in 1966, while she was working at the local Chevrolet dealership, two good-looking men came into the Fleet Department. Her boss introduced both of them to Susan, and she could tell by the way they looked at her that they were interested. Within a couple of days, Frank called and asked her to go out. When she told her boss about the invitation, he advised her not to go out with him. He said he had known him for many years and that he was quite a womanizer.

Susan at 19

Susan, nineteen at the time, saw this as a challenge. She accepted his offer to go out, knowing full well that he was more than twelve years older than her. The first date was like a whirlwind. It seemed like everywhere they went, everyone knew this man. Frank was charming, funny, and treated her kindly.

They continued to date almost every day, often staying up past midnight to talk even though she had to get to work by 6:30 a.m. She thought the long nights were worth it because he was charming her off her feet.

When her mother first met this man, she knew he would have only one thing on his mind: getting her daughter into bed. She warned her daughter, but Susan, being young and stupid, didn't listen to the warnings. The whole time they dated, Frank told Susan that he would never get married again since he had been married twice, and children were out of the question completely since he already had four. She should have seen these red flags and ended the relationship, but by this time it was too late. Susan had fallen madly in love—or what she thought was love.

Ten months later, Frank asked, "Would you want to move in with me? I love you and would like to spend more time with you."

Susan was shocked. She never thought he would tell her he loved her. After all, he had said he never wanted to get married again. She thought for a moment and said, "My family would never understand if I moved in with you. They're 'old country,' I'm afraid."

Frank didn't give up. "Why don't we go away for the weekend to Vegas? We can tell your parents that we got married while we were gone. Then they would be okay with us living together."

This should have been red flag No. 2, but she agreed to his crazy plan. After a long weekend in Las Vegas, they went to Susan's parents and lied to them that they were married.

Ann was totally devastated by this news. She was sure her daughter had made a big mistake because she knew what kind of a man Frank was. He was extremely controlling and possessive—a my-way-

or-the-highway type of guy. Susan was their only daughter, and now they were deprived of the opportunity to throw her a beautiful wedding.

Susan, terribly naive, went along with Frank's plan because he was affectionate and sweet. She had been craving this kind of male attention.

Ann and Leslie didn't say much more after hearing the news that their daughter had eloped in Las Vegas. They figured that as long as their daughter was happy, they would not interfere. They were also told by their new "son-in-law" that they were not to buy any gifts for Susan or him for any occasion, and they could come over only when they were invited. Ann and Leslie were finally in a financial position where they could give some nice gifts, but now they were forbidden to do so.

Susan and Frank moved away within a year and settled on the other side of the country in Little Rock, Arkansas. After three years, Susan realized that she could not go through life without having a child, so she told Frank how she felt. She had been patient, hoping that he loved her enough to want to marry her and have children, but he hadn't changed his mind up to this point.

Then one night, when Frank was totally inebriated—which was the way he often came home—he told her, "You can go ahead and get off the pill. You can have a baby since you want one so bad. It isn't fair to you not to have the baby you've always wanted."

He had more directives. "Oh, and make the arrangements for us to get married so that we can make this a legitimate baby. But I want you to know that I don't babysit, and I don't change diapers."

This should have been red flag No. 3, but Susan was so happy her dreams were coming true that she didn't care. She could get married and have the baby she always wanted.

Susan went to work immediately making plans for their quick wedding—and it was quick. The following weekend, they were married by a justice of the peace and had two of their friends stand up for them. It wasn't exactly the type of wedding most girls dream of, but all Susan could think of was the baby she was about to have.

Fortunately, she had no problem getting pregnant. Within ten months after their wedding, Susan gave birth to a beautiful baby girl and named her Rachael. Susan was happy beyond belief. She had everything she ever wanted—she was married, living in a beautiful new house, and raising a baby she had dreamed of.

Frank was actually showing some attention to Rachael. He really did love her, but he just didn't want to have anything to do with changing diapers or being alone with her.

Big Changes

Everything changed when Frank came home one day and told Susan, "Start packing. We're moving to New York City!"

Susan couldn't believe her ears. "Please don't make me move. I really like it here in Little Rock. I've finally found some good friends, and Rachael is only two years old. What will we do in New York?"

"When I say we're moving, we're moving. Now start packing! I have a good business opportunity in New York, and I'm not turning it down."

After a couple of months in Riverdale, New York, which is near Yonkers, finances became tight. The relationship started to show the strain. Frank was out drinking almost every night with his friends from work, leaving Susan and Rachael alone in a run-down brownstone with no transportation. Susan started getting anxiety attacks because she had no one to talk to. She was not allowed to make long distance phone calls or hire a babysitter, so she and Rachael were trapped in the house twenty-four hours a day.

They only stayed in New York six months, but during that time, Susan came very close to leaving her husband because he was becoming more and more demanding. They went through several stages in their marriage—rags to riches, then riches to rags. One day they were well off financially, and then suddenly, they were living off food stamps. The feast-or-famine finances were hard to deal with, but Susan had known poverty, so she could handle the hard times. She felt she had to stay strong for her child's sake.

They moved to Tulsa, Oklahoma, where Frank started his own company. This only lasted a couple of years, and they lost all their earthly possessions to the bank when the company folded. Desperate to find another business opportunity, they moved to Scottsdale, Arizona, to start all over again. They did manage to purchase a house with a small down-payment, but they had no furniture. They bought some used beds, a used table and chairs, and a black-and-white TV. Susan had to start babysitting other children during the day to help out with the finances.

Susan had stopped going to church, but now that she was raising a young girl, she wanted to pass down some Christian values. Over many long nights, she realized that it was God she was searching for. Through a business relationship, she met a wonderful Christian lady who introduced her to true Christianity. Susan started to go to church and Bible studies. In a short period of time, she committed her life to Christ and became "born again."

When Rachael was six, Susan had a second child that she called her "miracle baby"—Christina. Her second daughter should never have been conceived, according to several doctors who had told Susan that there was no way she could get pregnant again. Yet she prayed for another baby, and God answered her prayers. When Christina was just over a year old, Susan had to have a hysterectomy due to severe female problems, but Susan felt she had the perfect family.

Although she had her family, they moved to a different city or a different state almost every year, so it was hard to start or maintain any friendships. Frank became more and more possessive, if that was possible. As Susan got older and stronger, she started to fight back, which did not go over too well with him. Their fighting became more frequent.

Ann visited them once in a while, and she saw how Rachael was being disciplined by her father. She did not agree with his methods, but she was afraid to say anything for fear of getting thrown out of the house.

One incident stood out in her mind. During one of her visits when Rachael was about three, whenever Frank told Rachael to do something, she answered by saying, "Yes, Daddy."

This was not good enough for him, however. He demanded that she say, "Yes, sir!"

Rachael didn't understand why she couldn't say, "Yes, Daddy." When she disobeyed or didn't say, "Yes, sir," he scolded her or smacked her on her behind. Rachael would start crying because her feelings were hurt more than anything else. She was an extremely sensitive little girl.

It didn't help matters when Frank saw her crying. He yelled at her, "Straighten up that face, or I will give you something to really cry about!"

Rachael had to learn to hold all her feelings inside since she was not allowed to cry when punished. This caused her terrible anguish, and she became a withdrawn little girl who always agreed with her daddy.

When Christina was about the same age, she had quite a different personality. When she was told to straighten her face, she would say, "No." She refused to say, "No, sir" and "Yes, sir," and she always spoke her own mind, knowing full well that she would be punished, but she didn't care. She wasn't as afraid of her father as Rachael was, but there were times when he would yell at her so much that she finally had to give in.

Both girls would look to their mother for help, but Susan was afraid of getting into the middle of it, knowing what would happen if she ever interfered when he disciplined the children. She was weak and afraid of his wrath.

Meanwhile, Ann and Leslie didn't speak their minds. They felt sorry for Susan and knew that their daughter was not happy in her marriage.

After being gone for almost thirteen years, Frank and Susan moved the family back to California. Susan loved living close to her family again. They lived near Ann and Leslie for a while, and Ann was thrilled to have them back. Rachael and Christina were eight and two, and Ann looked forward to spoiling them on the weekends. She finally had her grandchildren nearby, so she would spoil them as much as she wanted to.

Rachael took ice-skating lessons and became quite good at spins and jumps, but then she discovered how much she really loved horses. Susan and Frank leased a horse that their daughter could ride and take care of each day. As Rachael's sixteenth birthday approached, they saw how much she loved riding and taking care of horses, so they bought her a horse of her very own.

Rachael could hardly wait for each school day to be over so she could go and spend time with her beloved horse. She groomed him daily, and on cold nights she would drive down to the stables to cover him. She won many ribbons for showing and jumping. When the time came for her to go off to college, she had to sell her horse and was heartbroken for months.

Ice Time

Christina tried ballet when she was around five, but that was not her talent. Then she started ice-skating with her sister, which she really loved. The two sisters enjoyed skating together and performed in several shows that the whole family attended.

When Christina was about a year old, Ann taught her how to swim. Ann had to take care of her for a couple of weeks when Susan had to be hospitalized. Since Ann and Leslie had a pool in their backyard, she felt it was necessary to teach Christina how to swim early—for safety reasons.

By the time she was six, Christina was competing in swim meets, and like Great Uncle Zoli, swimming became her passion. She gave up ice-skating and spent most of her free time training for her swim meets. Over the next several years, she won trophies, ribbons, and many awards for her excellent swimming skills. She also earned a college scholarship for swimming, but she turned it down because she was burned out by the time she graduated from high school. Besides being a swimmer, Christina was a cheerleader throughout high school as well. Even with her extracurricular activities, she earned good grades and graduated in the top thirty out of six-hundred in her class.

Christina, Rachael, Jessica - 2003

Since Rachael and Christina were doing well in school and had their own interests outside of school, Susan spent many hours volunteering at their church. Frank continued to work hard to get ahead, and to everyone on the outside, they looked like the perfect little family. Ann and Leslie picked up on the friction between Susan and Frank, however, which concerned them, but they never said anything.

As the girls reached their teenage years, Susan decided that she wanted to have a career. After discussing the matter with Frank and trying to impress upon him how important this was to her, he agreed that she could start gemology school.

Susan was the oldest of twenty-eight students, but that did not bother her or the students. She got along with everyone. The courses were extremely challenging with homework every night and quizzes every morning. The school was over an hour away from their house, so Susan was gone most of the day. Nonetheless, Frank still expected her to have dinner on the table at a certain time, keep the house clean, and get all the errands done just as she had done before.

She passed all her exams the first time, which led to a job offer in a fine jewelry store the day she graduated. She started working within a couple of weeks and really enjoyed talking with people about beautiful jewelry. According to her supervisor, Susan was a natural at selling expensive pieces.

She and a co-worker, Elaine, arrived at work one Wednesday morning in time to open the doors at 10 o'clock. The store had only been open for one hour when two African-American men walked through the mall, entered the store, and walked toward the back where Susan and Elaine were.

"Is there something we can help you gentlemen with?" Susan asked.

One of the men pulled out a revolver from his pants and pointed it at Susan's forehead. He calmly said, "Yes, you can help me by filling up my bag with jewelry."

Then he pointed the gun at Elaine. "Get in the back and lay down on the floor face down!"

Susan's heart leaped to her throat. "Where do you want me to start?" she asked.

The other man immediately locked the front door, went in the back room, pulled the phone cord out of the wall, and removed the security tape from the recorder.

The man with the revolver told Susan to walk over to the display window. "Open the window and start putting everything into my bag!"

Susan's hands were shaking so hard that she could not get the key into the tiny hole. The delay annoyed the robber. He screamed at her, "Get the damn window open, or I'll shoot you right here!"

"I'm trying, but I can't seem to get it open!" cried Susan. She was finally able to open the display window and started pulling necklaces and rings off the displays. The most valuable pieces were displayed in the window, so Susan was extra careful not to harm any of the jewelry.

But that infuriated the robber. "Don't take them off the displays. Just grab as much as you can with two hands and throw them into the bag!"

As soon as she emptied the display window, he told her to go to the back of the store where they kept all the platinum jewelry. Apparently the robbers had "cased the joint" a few days before because he knew exactly which case had the platinum. Susan walked behind the counter, and the robber walked in front of it, keeping his eyes on her the whole time.

As Susan passed by the counter with the silent alarm, she reached under and pushed the button as quickly as she possibly could. When the robber saw her make a strange move, that angered him. "What did you just do? Did you just press a button?"

Susan was terrified. "No, I didn't press anything, I was just adjusting my skirt."

The robber came behind the counter to see for himself. While looking under the counter, he saw a button and knew what she had done.

He jammed his handgun into Susan's temple and screamed, "You pushed the silent alarm, you bitch! Get in the back of the store and get on the floor!"

Susan turned with a heaviness in her heart that she had never known before. She felt that this was it. This man was definitely going to kill her and Elaine.

She went to the back room and lay on top of Elaine. She didn't know what else to do but pray. She figured if she was going to die, at least she would go out praying, so she began to pray out loud, expecting a bullet to strike at any second.

A few minutes went by, and nothing happened. Elaine said to Susan, "Let's get up and see where they are. I think they've gone!"

They both stood up very quietly and looked around the small room and saw no one. When they walked out to the showroom, they saw that they were alone. Nobody was around. Immediately Susan ran to lock the front door, and Elaine called the police on the phone in the display area.

Then they huddled in a corner, still trembling from the events that just happened and hoping the police would arrive soon. The police showed up within ten minutes and took their statements. They discovered that the silent alarm had not worked. Susan almost got killed for nothing, but she was thankful to be alive. The owners of the store thanked her for trying to call for help, and they also realized that Susan had saved them a lot of money because the robbers never did get any of the platinum jewelry.

When her family found out what had happened, they were grateful that Susan was not murdered. Ann could not have survived losing one of her children, especially under such violent circumstances.

It took Susan a while to get over the robbery, but she had become used to bad things happening to her. Her only comfort was her faith. She knew she could have been shot, but God had saved her. She was thankful for His protection and that it wasn't her time to go yet.

A Significant Turn Is Made

Frank's behavior became worse whenever Susan stood up for herself and challenged him. At the far end of inappropriate, of course, was the physical abuse, which only happened once. The real damage was caused by emotional distance and indifference. Frank was slowly wearing her down with manipulation and subtle verbal insults, constantly criticizing her actions, questioning her whereabouts, and demanding to know how every penny was spent.

He had great jobs, and most people liked him because he could be charming in his own way. Frank was certainly a hard worker and good friend to many. But something was off about him.

Some of their friends noticed his odd behavior at social gatherings, and Susan's friends tried to warn her about it. At home, he would turn from being a kindly Dr. Jekyll—loving and attentive one minute—to a Mr. Hyde the next minute when he would blow up and call her filthy names. Then he would blame Susan for his erratic behavior, which made her think there was something seriously wrong with *her*.

After many years, she realized that his behavior was not her fault. Frank mistakenly directed his anger at her for *his* insecurities and childhood traumas. After a while, Susan realized that forgiving him one more time and crawling back would solve nothing.

The marriage finally ended in divorce after almost thirty years, and to add insult to injury, they also filed for bankruptcy, leaving Susan only her sanity. She hung in there as long as she could, as she had seen her mother do, but Susan never realized that permanent damage was being done to her girls while they were growing up in a dysfunctional family. At least Susan had the nerve to divorce him and help herself before it was too late.

At the same time, she mourned the death of her marriage. The thirty-two years she had spent with Frank were a big chunk of her life—at this point more than half her life. She tried to understand what went wrong and why she had absolutely no feelings left for this man. She believed that her former husband needed to control their relationship completely. To maintain control he was verbally, if not physically, abusive.

Frank had degraded her, resented any outside interests she had, and had become furious for trivial reasons. Susan had grown up with extremely low self-esteem because of the way her father had treated her, which explained why she was drawn to Frank. He had been extremely charming and devoted at times, but also extremely domineering at other times.

He was definitely the type to take charge in any given situation, but as the years went by, Susan realized that this bullying attitude was merely an attempt to conceal his insecurities. Susan could not understand how her husband could be so wonderful one minute and so vicious the next, even though he claimed that he would be nice all the time if she would only change and behave like he wanted her to.

Susan was told by a marriage counselor that the man she married was a misogynist. She also explained to Susan that these relationships can be saved only if the man realizes how he got this way and is willing to do a huge amount of work to change his behavior toward his intimate partner. If he cannot do this, then the relationship cannot be saved.

Susan developed anxiety and depression while waiting for him to change. She finally realized that it was not worth her health to try to change a man who harbored a deep resentment toward women, especially women with a brain in their heads. If it had not been for her faith in God and the strength she drew from Him, she would have not lasted as long as she did. Years after the divorce, she concluded that she really could not blame him as much as she blamed herself for allowing him to treat her the way he did since Frank had not forced her to stay against her will.

One thing Susan was grateful for was becoming a much stronger person through this relationship, and she would do it over again to have her two girls who meant everything to her. She realized too late that she should have ended the marriage much sooner.

Susan and her mother, Ann, talked about their marriages, and they came to the conclusion that their husbands were very much alike. Susan had basically married the same type of man that her mother had married. Their husbands were both several years older than their wives, they were controlling, they were interested in inappropriate sexual activities, and they were possessive and jealous.

But all those bad experiences were left in the past as Susan moved toward a brighter future.

19

Nick's Adventures

*A*fter Nick finished his studies in electrome-
chanical engineering at Long Beach State, he
immediately found a position at Northrop, a defense
firm. He then moved on to larger companies like
Electronic Memories & Magnetics and Litton Indus-
tries.

He had worked hard to get his education, which he
paid for himself. Nick worked at several different jobs
to put himself through school. He repaired electronic
equipment at Radio Shack and repaired cameras at
Firestone Camera. He also built and repaired naviga-
tion equipment for small aircraft at Condor Pacific.

He was dedicated to all his jobs, displaying a passion for mechanical engineering and anything to do
with electronic gadgets. With such a bright future,
he was able to move out of the apartment he shared
with his family and get his own apartment after a
few months. He started dating different women and
had a couple of serious relationships, but they didn't

work out. As he was getting close to thirty, he started thinking that it was time to look for a wife.

He decided that he would go back to Hungary to visit his relatives. Perhaps he could find a nice Hungarian girl in the old country. He made travel plans, but after talking to his mother, he realized that it would be a great idea to go to Austria first and look up the lady who helped Ann years ago when she was pregnant with him.

Ann told Nick, "Go surprise her. Here's her address. Hopefully she still lives there. People in little towns don't move around that much. Tell her I think of her often and of her generosity and kindness toward us."

When Nick arrived in St. Michael, Austria, he found the small peasant house that his mother had described. He knocked on the door, and an older gentleman opened it.

He was welcomed into the house. Suddenly an old lady screamed out, "Nicholas, you have come!"

Nick was shocked, to say the least. He wanted to surprise her, but she called him by name after not seeing him since he was two weeks old—almost thirty years ago. With the help of a translator, he found out that the old woman had a dream six weeks earlier about Nick coming to visit her. That's why she knew it was him.

After spending a few hours visiting, the lady informed Nick that she had two granddaughters. Either one of them would make a great wife for Nick, she said, but he declined respectfully.

Upon arriving in Hungary, he immediately went to Debrecen, the city where Ann and Leslie met. Most of his cousins and his paternal grandmother lived there, so he made that his first stop. One of his cousins, who was about the same age as Nick, asked one of his friends to come by the house.

"I want you to meet Ildy. She is my best friend," said András.

Nick shook Ildy's hand. "Very nice to meet you," he said.

She looked to be about sixteen. *I wish she was older,* he thought. *She sure is cute!*

Nick pulled András aside. "What are you doing hanging out with a sixteen-year-old?"

András laughed. "Ildy is twenty. She just looks young."

Nick was happy to hear this. *Oh, that changes things!*

He immediately took a liking to her, and they spent the next day together. They got along so well and had so much fun that Nick planned to ask Ildy to marry him after knowing her for only twenty-four hours. When he took her home that night around ten o'clock, Ildy introduced him to her parents, who checked him out from top to bottom. They were suspicious. *Who is this American young man, and what does he want with our little girl?*

The four of them sat around and talked for hours. Around one o'clock in the morning, Nick popped the big question: "Will you please give me permission to marry your daughter? I love her, and I want to spend the rest of my life with her."

Ildy's father was speechless, but he composed himself. "You only met yesterday. Why don't you wait a little while before you start thinking about marriage? Do you think we are going to let our one and only daughter go to America with a total stranger?"

After checking into the requirements for leaving the country due to marriage, Nick and Ildy discovered that the Hungarian government would not let her leave for one year. Nick returned to the U.S. by himself. Now very much in love, they stayed the course and were married within a year, but the ceremony had to be in Hungary, according to their rules. As soon as it was possible, Ildy came to the U.S. after receiving her visa and other necessary documents.

Nick and Ildy's Wedding in Hungary - 1975

They had a child within a few years and named her Jessica. When she was about five, she was diagnosed with a rare form of thyroid cancer. Nick and Ildy were told that there were four types of thyroid cancer, and Jessica had a version called follicular cancer, one of the most aggressive forms. The cancer cells invade the blood vessels, then travel to other parts of the body. In her case, the cancer was in her thyroid and trachea and behind her vocal cords. There was also a large tumor next to her lung.

The doctors did not think she would make it and informed her parents that their only child would probably not survive. If she did pull through, she would never talk again because her vocal cords would be compromised because of the cancerous tissue behind them.

The family was devastated. Ann, Leslie, Susan, and Frank prayed continually and requested that everyone in their churches pray also. Susan's daughter, Rachael, who was thirteen at the time, took it upon herself to call the Prayer Tower in Tulsa, Oklahoma, so they could put Jessica on their prayer list.

When her dad came home, Rachael walked up to him. She was scared to death and said, "Daddy, I know you're going to get mad because I just made a long distance call."

"Where did you call?" Frank asked.

"I called the Prayer Tower in Tulsa so they can all pray for Jessica. I'm sorry."

Instead of being mad, Frank and Susan started crying. All they could do was hug Rachael and love her for being so thoughtful at the age of thirteen.

The whole family spent Thanksgiving at the hospital. Frank and Susan had a travel trailer, which they drove to the hospital parking lot. Ann and Susan prepared delicious dishes at home and brought them to the trailer, where they had a Thanksgiving feast and took turns going up to see Jessica.

Jessica had made a paper turkey in the hospital with the other kids, and the family proudly displayed the homemade craft as their centerpiece at the family dinner. Everyone in the family felt this was the most wonderful Thanksgiving of their lives!

Jessica endured several surgeries, and after the fourth, the surgeon walked out of the operating room and said, "I don't know what happened in there, but we had help. Jessica will be fine, but we'll have to see how her voice recovers in a few days."

Jessica had to receive radioactive iodine to kill off any cancer cells that might be left in her body. Since she was only five, they gave it to her in a liquid form. Everyone had to clear the room, and a nurse dressed in an asbestos suit came in and handed Jessica a small cup. This liquid was extremely radioactive, and the toilet had to be flushed seven times after she used it.

A few minutes after she drank the medicine, Jessica started vomiting profusely. The family stood helplessly outside a glass window since they were forbidden from entering the room. Ildy screamed for help, and the family begged one of the nurses to go in and help Jessica. No one dared to enter the room, so Ann took it upon herself to rush in and help her grandchild, who was scared to death.

Ann took a washcloth and cleaned her up the best she could. Then she sat and held Jessica and comforted her. When the nurses found out what had happened, they sent in a technician to check how much radiation Ann had received. They knew both her arms had been affected because the Geiger counter beeped like crazy. Ann was told that she had a chance of getting cancer within twenty years because of the amount of radioactivity.

Jessica's voice returned after a couple of days, and within several weeks she was back to normal. Jessica grew up to be a healthy young woman and even participated in beauty pageants as a teenager, winning a few. She got married and has two beautiful children.

Losing Out

Nick and Ildy's relationship had been strained for many years during and after Jessica's illness. When something tragic happens to a child, the parents sometimes unconsciously blame each other and seek attention elsewhere. In many instances, the marriage suffers terribly. This is exactly what happened to Nick and Ildy.

Nick spent many hours working overtime to keep busy and keep his mind off Jessica. Ildy joined a support group for women to help her overcome her pain, but many of the women were bitter toward their husbands. She became discouraged listening to their critical and sarcastic remarks.

Nick eventually started his own company and sunk every dime into the new business. Ildy worked with him, and the company thrived for several years until they noticed several strange and unexplainable events. Some of their customers wouldn't return their calls, and others stopped doing business with them for no apparent reason. As it turned out, two employees in high positions, whom Nick trusted, were stealing customers and steering them toward their own side businesses. By the time this became known to Nick and Ildy, it was too late to turn things around. They lost their company to a couple of swindlers.

This turn of events was more than Nick could bear. First his daughter had been seriously ill, then his marriage had faltered, his own health wasn't the greatest, and now people he trusted had betrayed him. He was disillusioned and wondered, *How much more can I take?*

He finally went back to work in his field within a few months and started to regain some of his pride. He had to retire at an early age, however, due to several health issues. His marriage to Ildy survived all the challenges they faced.

After witnessing how they had made it through some bad times, Nick's mother couldn't understand why her son and his wife did not believe in anything spiritual. One time, Ann asked Nick, "Do you believe in a Supreme Being?"

His reply was no, but he pondered the question for a while. Even though he attended Holy Ghost

Catholic School after arriving in Canada and went to Mass on Sundays, he left the church when he got out on his own. At one time he had tried to put Christian beliefs into scientific terms, but it was an impossible stretch for him.

Nick told his mother, "I now realize that I am not an atheist. I am really an agnostic, as many scientists are. I believe that evidence must be presented before something can be believed, and a scientist only deals with the facts. This is my identity. As for the future, I will believe if God can be proven scientifically."

Nick's unbelief and criticism of Christians grew more intense as the years passed. Anyone who believed that AIDS, cancer, bacteria, or viruses were intelligently designed was fooling themselves, and he refused to believe in a Higher Power. He constantly brought up the subject to Ann and Susan every chance he got, wanting to debate. He would put down Christianity whenever the family got together, which strained his relationship with them. He even demanded that the prayer before a meal be stopped in his presence because it made him and his wife uncomfortable.

Susan gave up debating the issue, but she remained strong in her convictions that Jesus Christ is the Son of God, and it is only through believing in Him that one can gain eternal life. She decided to be an example of a true Christian woman by loving her brother and continually praying for him with the hope that someday he would see the light. Ildy, who was raised in a Communist country and taught about atheism, agrees with her husband. She, too, is convinced that God does not exist.

Nick and Ildy have both discouraged their daughter, Jessica, from believing in Jesus, even though she attended Sunday school as a young girl and listened to Aunt Susan read Bible stories. Jessica has chosen to follow the path set by her parents. Susan believes that the only thing she can do is pray for Jessica and her family and then pray some more.

Their non-belief has broken Ann's heart because she and the family have experienced unexplainable miracles and felt God's hand in their lives. Ann was pleased when Susan, in her early twenties, realized that she had a void in her life that only God could fill.

This mother who miraculously escaped from Hungary continues to pray for Nick and his family and has given the matter over to the Lord.

20

Peace at Last

*A*fter Leslie's funeral in the fall of 2009, Ann had an extremely tough season of life and waited a few months before doing the inevitable. She had to go through Leslie's clothes and personal belongings, which brought back memories of certain events in their lives—and some of them were not pleasant. She mourned her husband and even missed him. After all, sixty-five years is a long time to spend with one person.

Leslie was now at peace, and Ann comforted herself with the knowledge that he was not tormented by his demons any longer. She also reminded herself that Leslie could not hurt her anymore.

After Susan divorced Frank in 1998, she lived by herself in a one-bedroom apartment for two years. She loved every minute of her solitude. She came to the realization that everyone has a choice regarding the attitude he or she will embrace for that day. She could not change the past. She could not change the fact that people act in a certain way, and she could not change the inevitable. The only thing she could do was to keep a positive attitude. This knowledge kept her burdens light. She could go on with life when she let go of her heartaches.

Things were tough financially at first since she got nothing out of the divorce. The bankruptcy didn't help matters. Susan was fortunate to land a job and budgeted every penny, but her salary was barely enough to pay the bills. She had her degree as a gemologist, but she had to leave the jewelry business because she could not afford to work on commission any longer.

One time Susan was listening to radio show host and Christian author Chuck Swindoll, and he said something that caught her attention: "People who soar are those who refuse to sit back, sigh, and wish things would change. They neither complain of their lot nor passively dream of some distant ship coming in. Rather, they visualize in their minds that they are not quitters and will not allow life's circumstances to push them down and hold them under."

She had her health, she had her girls, and she was looking forward to a new future. All her friends she had acquired through the last twenty years were special to her, and she wasn't concerned they would turn their back on her now that she was single and broke.

Susan was overwhelmed by their friendship through her tough times, and their concern and support helped her get through. They never excluded her from any of heir parties, even though she was single, which meant the world to her. They proved that they were friends by not abandoning her when things got tough.

Some of those friends tried to set her up with a nice man, but she wanted no part of it. She was scared of the whole dating scene.

Finally, after being single for a couple of years, Susan went to a Christian singles dance on the *Queen Mary*, an old British ocean liner docked in Long Beach. Around 1,200 singles were in attendance. Susan had been praying to meet a nice Christian man who was tall, about her age, and in control of his temper. God says to be specific when you pray, so she got specific in what she was looking for in a man.

She didn't really want to get married again, but she was open to finding a companion to share her life with. At the *Queen Mary* that night, she saw a tall, good-looking man at the dance, and after a few eye contacts and smiles, he asked her to dance. They talked and danced the rest of the night. She found out that his name was Steve Van Loon. He was a firefighter, his father had been a policeman, and he had one sister and a loving mother. He asked for her phone number when he left the dance, and she excitedly waited for him to call.

After she had told all her friends that she had met this nice man, they phoned her daily to see if he had called. Susan was getting embarrassed to say that he still hadn't called yet, but finally, two weeks later on a Saturday afternoon, her phone rang.

"Hi," said the deep voice. "Do you remember me? This is Steve, and we met at the Christian singles dance on the *Queen Mary* a couple of weeks ago."

Susan pretended that she really didn't know who he was. "Are you the tall man with gray hair?" she asked.

"That would be me," he answered. "I'm sorry I haven't called sooner, but I had plans to go on a cruise. Then I visited my mother in the desert. Now I'm free. I was wondering if you wanted to go out with me some time?"

Susan's heart started beating fast. "I guess that would be all right. When did you have in mind?"

"Well, I'm working now and will be off by five o'clock. I could meet you around 6:30. Will that be all right?"

Susan was petrified at the thought of dating at her age. She had heard horror stories of women getting caught in situations they could not control. She thought about it for a minute and then remembered a restaurant that was close to her parents. He agreed to meet her there at the appointed time. Then Susan called her mother and told her where she would be — just in case.

Courting Time

Susan and Steve both arrived at the same time and talked for a while before they ordered their food. When their salad arrived, Steve asked if she minded if he prayed and gave thanks for the food. She was shocked! This is not what she had heard about single men!

She had been told that bachelors wanted only one thing out of any relationship, so they would wine and dine a woman to get what they were after. This man was different. Not only did he seem sincere, he wanted to talk about spiritual matters and what he was learning in the Bible. They talked for many hours that evening and saw each other every weekend after that since he lived fifty miles from where she lived.

After seeing Steve a few times, Susan, during a routine checkup, was told she had thyroid cancer and should undergo surgery soon. She didn't think it was fair to Steve to have to deal with this, so she drove to his house to talk to him. She had called to let him know that she needed to see him.

After opening the door and greeting her, he asked, "Is everything all right?"

"No, it's not," she replied. "I just found out that I have thyroid cancer and will have to undergo surgery in a few weeks. I wanted to let you know and tell you that it's all right if you don't want to see me again."

His blue eyes got huge. Steve came over and sat next to her. "Friends don't leave each other when there is a problem. I will be with you through this whole thing. You can depend on me."

He held her hand and asked, "Is it all right if I pray for you now?"

She was taken aback by his request, not believing her ears. "I would love that. Thank you very much."

Susan's thyroid cancer was not the aggressive form that Jessica had. Susan had been diagnosed with papillary thyroid cancer, which is the least invasive to the body. Her cancer was enclosed in a nodule that sat on top of her thyroid, so the whole thyroid and the nodule had to be removed. The doctors had told Ann when she helped Jessica years ago that she could possibly get cancer within twenty years, but it was Susan who ended up with it.

Susan had her surgery, and Steve was there with a dozen red roses, along with her family and friends waiting for her to wake up from her anesthesia. While she was recovering, she stayed with Ann and Leslie, who lived much closer to Steve's house, so he came to visit her every day. They took slow walks, played cards, or just watched TV while she recovered. Ann was convinced that the concern and care that Steve showed for Susan was a definite factor in her fast recovery.

After a few months, Susan started to realize that this man was exactly what she had been praying for—even though she had not prayed for good looking—God just threw that in as an extra bonus. After seeing each other for a year and a half, they were walking in a park in Pasadena, killing time before they went to a Christmas party.

They were throwing a ball to each other, giggling and laughing, when Steve suddenly stopped and asked, "Would you do me a big favor?"

Susan had no idea what he meant. "Of course, just tell me what you want."

"Will you marry me?" he blurted out.

Susan's heart leaped. She had no idea this was coming. She had assumed that they would just remain good friends since he had never been married before.

"I would love to marry you!" Then she started crying, and as her lips quivered, they hugged for the longest time. Then they kissed and laughed in joy.

Susan had not dated any other man since her divorce. She ended up marrying Steve six months to the day after he proposed on June 22, 2002.

Susan and Steve's Wedding in California - 2002

Susan is now at peace. She has her "Gentle Giant" who truly loves her. Steve never abuses her in any way, treats her like a queen, and says things like, "My goal in life is to make you happy."

And she is happy. They have so much in common beyond their belief in Christ. They play tennis, they golf, they play cards, and they love the outdoors. Now that they are both retired, they are together every day and don't tire of each other's company. Susan is looking forward to growing old with Steve.

New Families Forming

Susan's daughters are both married, and Susan is thrilled that both of them married the "perfect man" for them. When Christina was dating her husband, Andrew, he told her, "I predict that you and I will be married within a year, and in a couple of years we will have twin boys. Then we'll have a little girl."

Christina blinked twice. "That sure is a lot to hope for. Don't you think that's pushing it? But I sure hope you're right because it sounds like the perfect family scenario to me!"

"You'll see," said Andrew.

They both forgot about this prediction until years later—after twin boys Aiden and Gavin were born. The twins were followed a couple of years later by a beautiful baby girl Isabella. Then it hit them that Andrew's prediction had come true, and they now had the family they had always wanted.

Rachael was very particular about the men she dated. She was looking for a certain kind of man and would not settle for just anyone. He had to be like her in many ways. She was in her early thirties when she met David through her best friend, and they hit it off from the first moment. They had so much in common and could not stop talking for hours after they met. They dated for a few months, and they both knew this was right, so David asked her to marry him. They are like two peas in a pod. They love each other, adore their children, and have created a wonderful life together.

Susan's girls have great careers. Christina is an ultrasound technologist, and Rachael puts her master's degree in psychology to good use at her present job. They juggle their careers and being moms beautifully.

Great-grandchildren, twins Aiden and Gavin

Ann's great granddaughter, Isabella

Great granddaughters, Charlotte and Olivia

Susan had prayed through all their early years for a good husband for each of them, and He has provided that. Rachael has two children, and Christina has three, so Susan is the proud grandmother of five beautiful grandchildren. The only problem is that Susan can only see her girls once a year since they both live so far away, but that makes it even more special when they get together.

Nick is happy in his new life as well. He and Ildy bought a new house on top of a mountain near Tehachapi in Central California. There's plenty of land. Nick loves to work outdoors since he had to work in an office all his life. He is constantly building something, and they have a vineyard, a chicken coop, a hot house, an orchard with many different fruit trees, and beautiful flower gardens to tend to.

Their daughter Jessica has two beautiful girls, Charlotte and Olivia. She and her husband, Ryan, love them dearly and spend as much time with them as possible. Jessica is quite the cook and used to have her own catering business. Now she's home with her children, but she still has time to put out wonderful recipes on Facebook.

Zoli never did find the happiness he was looking for. He was always a dreamer and always had the "perfect" business opportunity around the corner. Nothing ever panned out for him, however, and he ended up with few earthly possessions in his old age. He was always chasing rainbows to gain wealth, but he never saw how rich he was just by being blessed with his children and family.

His sister, Ann, is helping him out financially. Zoli was always there for the family when he was younger, so Ann feels obligated to help him. She has a heart of gold, a forgiving heart, and she has always taken care of her family, no matter what sacrifices she had to make.

Today, Ann is at peace with herself, with her Lord, and she has everything she has ever wanted. Her husband has been gone since 2009, and she is enjoying the solitude. The resentment she felt toward Leslie before his death has been slowly fading away with time, and now she tries to remember only the good parts of their marriage.

She finally let go of the anger that was like acid burning away the delicate layers of her happiness. She does not have to cater to anyone and can think about herself for a change. Ann has a beautiful home that's paid for, and she plays bridge with her friends several times a week and swims several times a week to stay fit. She also has Susan and Nick's total devotion and love. Her life has always been dedicated to her children, and now she is getting it back twofold. Her children love her and spend as much time as they can with her.

Ann loves her three granddaughters and her seven great-grandchildren, and she has pictures of her family throughout her home. As she wanders through the different rooms in her house, she is reminded of Rachael, her oldest granddaughter, in each room. Rachael has always given her meaningful gifts and things she made with her own hands. These mementos are special to Ann.

Susan, Ann and Nick - 2010

She has one particular gift from Rachael that she reads almost on a daily basis. It is a picture of Rachael's daughter, at two years of age, walking on a sidewalk next to footprints that were made when the asphalt was wet. Below it, Rachael wrote the story known as "Footprints," and had it matted and framed beautifully.

FOOTPRINTS

One night I dreamed I was walking along the
beach with the Lord.
Many scenes from my life flashed across the sky.
In each scene I noticed footprints in the sand,
Sometimes there were two set of
footprints in the sand,
other times there was only one set of footprints.

This bothered me because I noticed
that during the low periods of my life,
when I was suffering from anguish, sorrow or defeat,
I could see only one set of footprints.

So I said to the Lord,
"You promised me Lord that if I followed you,
you would walk with me always.
But I have noticed that during the most trying
periods of my life
there have only been one set of footprints in the sand.
Why, when I needed you most, you have
not been there for me?"

The Lord replied,
"The times when you have seen only one set of foot-
prints in the sand
is when I carried you."

Mary Stevenson

These poetic verses sum up Ann Szegedi's life, which is why this book is really about *her* story. Ann is grateful to her Lord for being there for her when she really needed strength and courage.

Although her life went from riches to rags, she now has all the riches she ever dreamed of.

With many Thanks,

t o **Mike Yorkey** who took time out of his busy schedule to edit my book; to **Catherine Martin** whose enthusiasm kept me going; to **Kelly Truitt** who dropped everything when I needed help; to **Diane King PhD** for her words of wisdom; to my husband, **Steve**, whose love, patience and support has been a tremendous comfort. Most of all I want to thank my mother, **Ann**, who is eighty-seven years old now, for her perseverance and her stamina in re-living her past experiences--some of which were not pleasant--then providing me with material in her hand-written Hungarian notes.

THE WHITE HOUSE

WASHINGTON

October 17, 1988

I am honored to commemorate with you the 32nd anniversary
of the Hungarian Revolution, which will be marked on
October 23. We can never forget the shining example of
the many brave men and women who faced death fearlessly
in 1956 to regain freedom and self-determination for their
beloved homeland. Their idealism, patriotism, and courage
remain an inspiration to all Hungarians who yearn for
freedom and democracy, as well as to other peoples around
the world who are engaged in the same struggle for their
countries.

The United States remains fully committed to the goals of
democracy, national self-determination, and human rights
for which the brave freedom fighters of 1956 fought.
These goals are timeless, and the struggle to achieve
them will continue as long as the desire for freedom rests
in the human heart. Today, when we hear much about
change and "new thinking" in the Eastern bloc, we hope
that leaders in that part of the world will take a new
look at the Hungarian Revolution and recognize the lessons
it carries to the present day. The situation in Europe
can never be considered normal until the cruel and unnatural
division of that continent is healed, and until historical
injustices such as the brutal suppression of the Hungarian
Revolution are forthrightly dealt with in the history books.
I remain convinced that that day will come, and I hope
and pray that it is not far in the future.

God bless you.

Ronald Reagan

CPSIA information can be obtained at www.ICGtesting.com
Printed in the USA
BVOW080357081112

304994BV00001B/1/P

9 781624 197864